THIS BOOK BELONGS TO

NAME:
AGE:
ADDRESS:

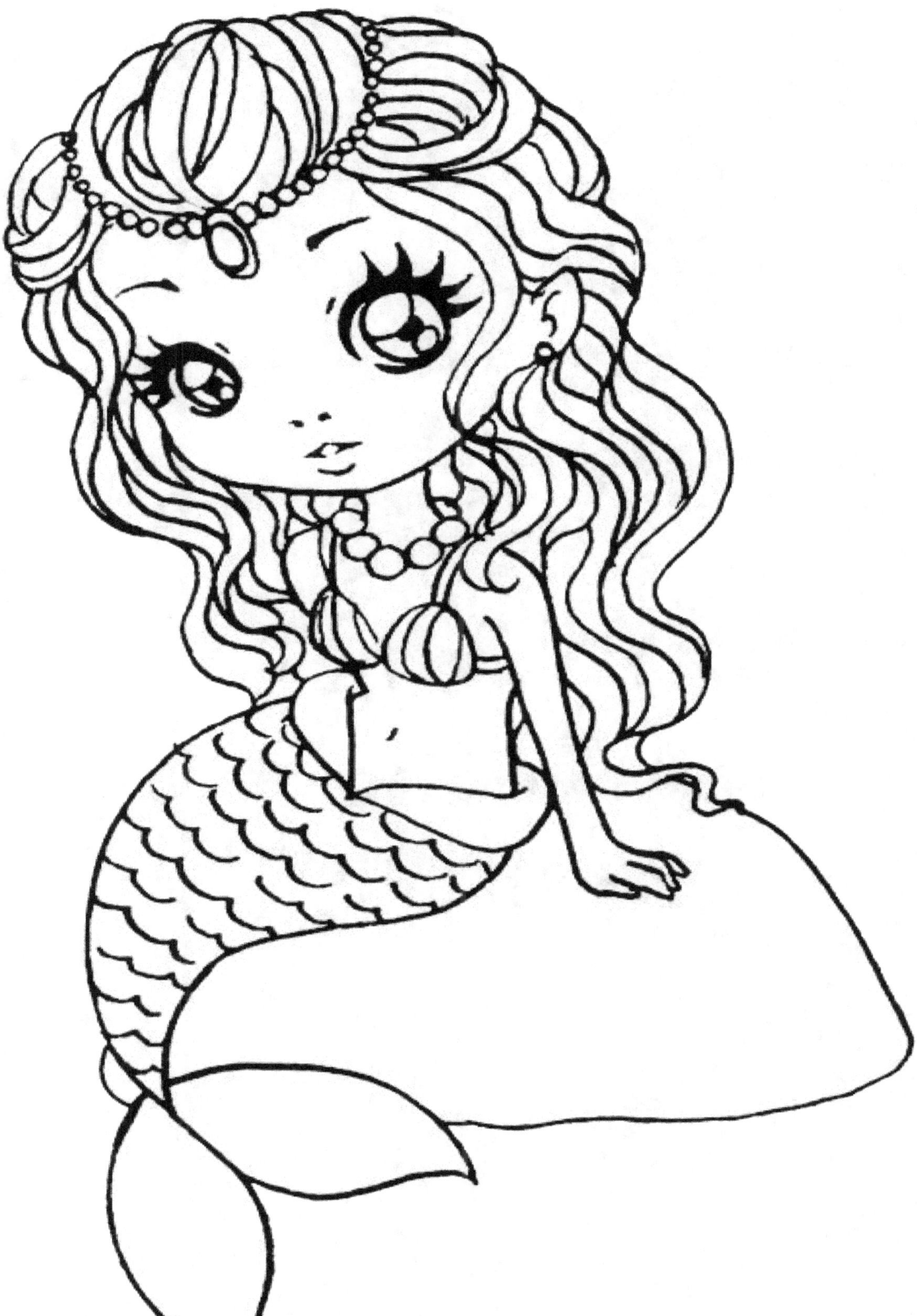

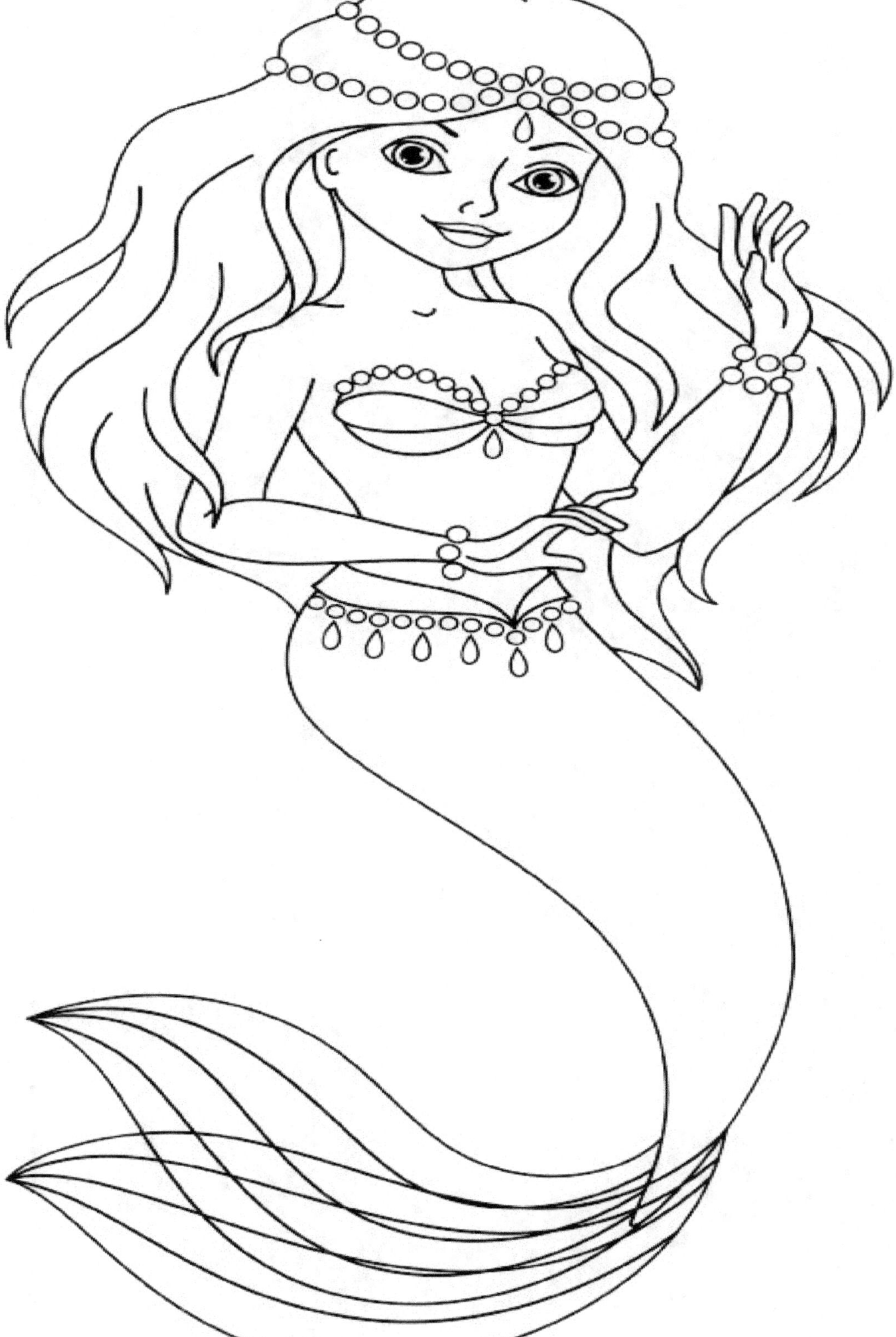

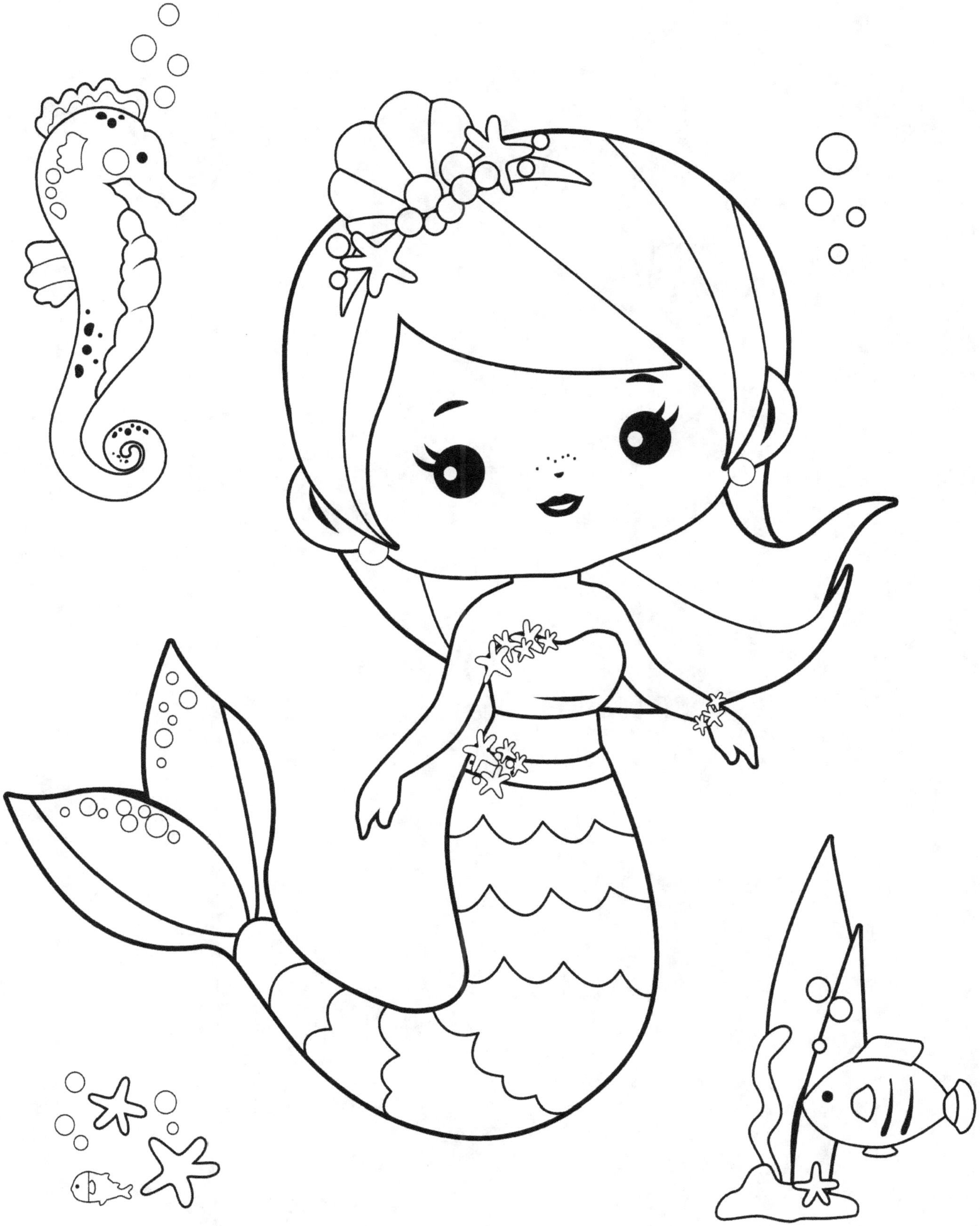

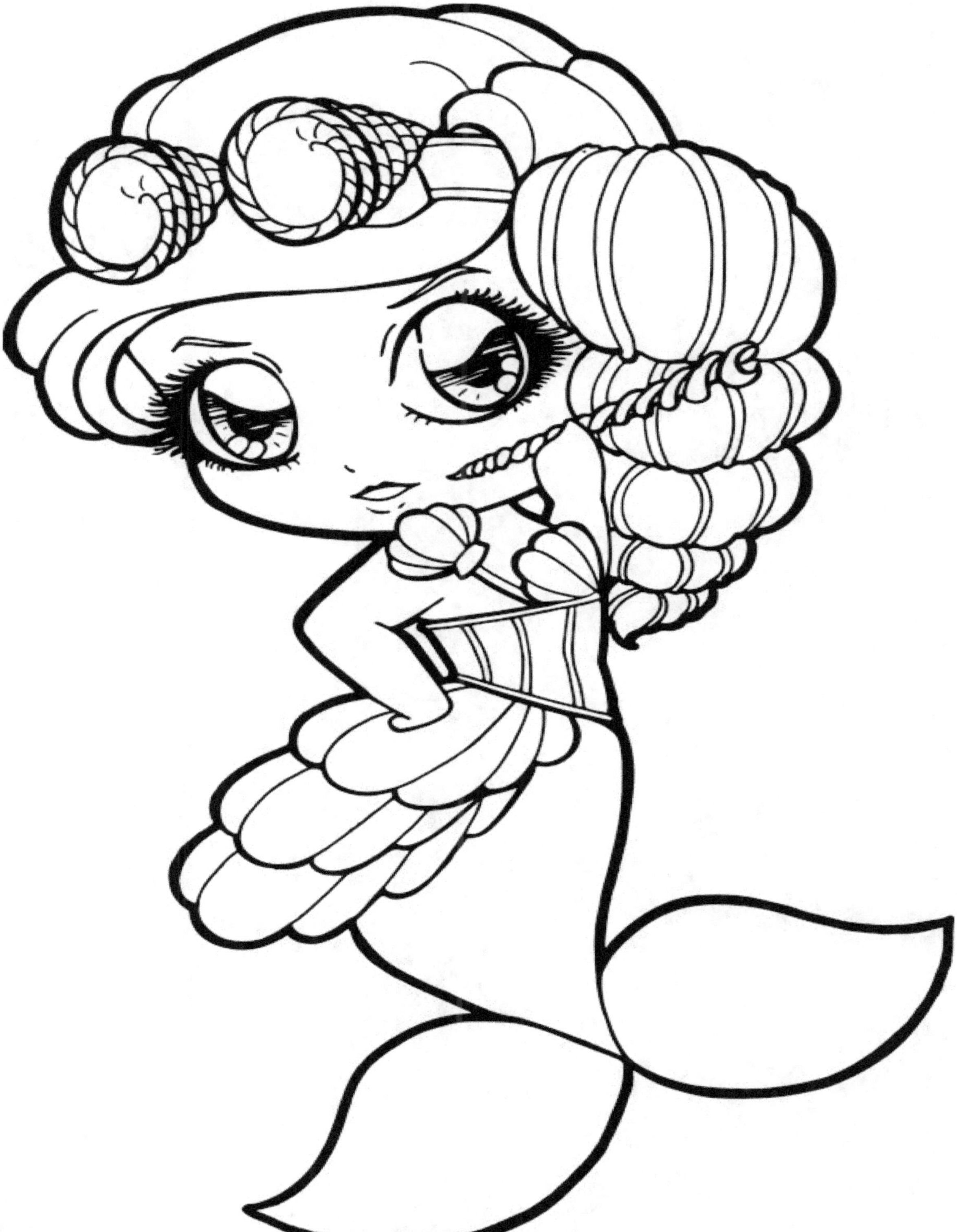

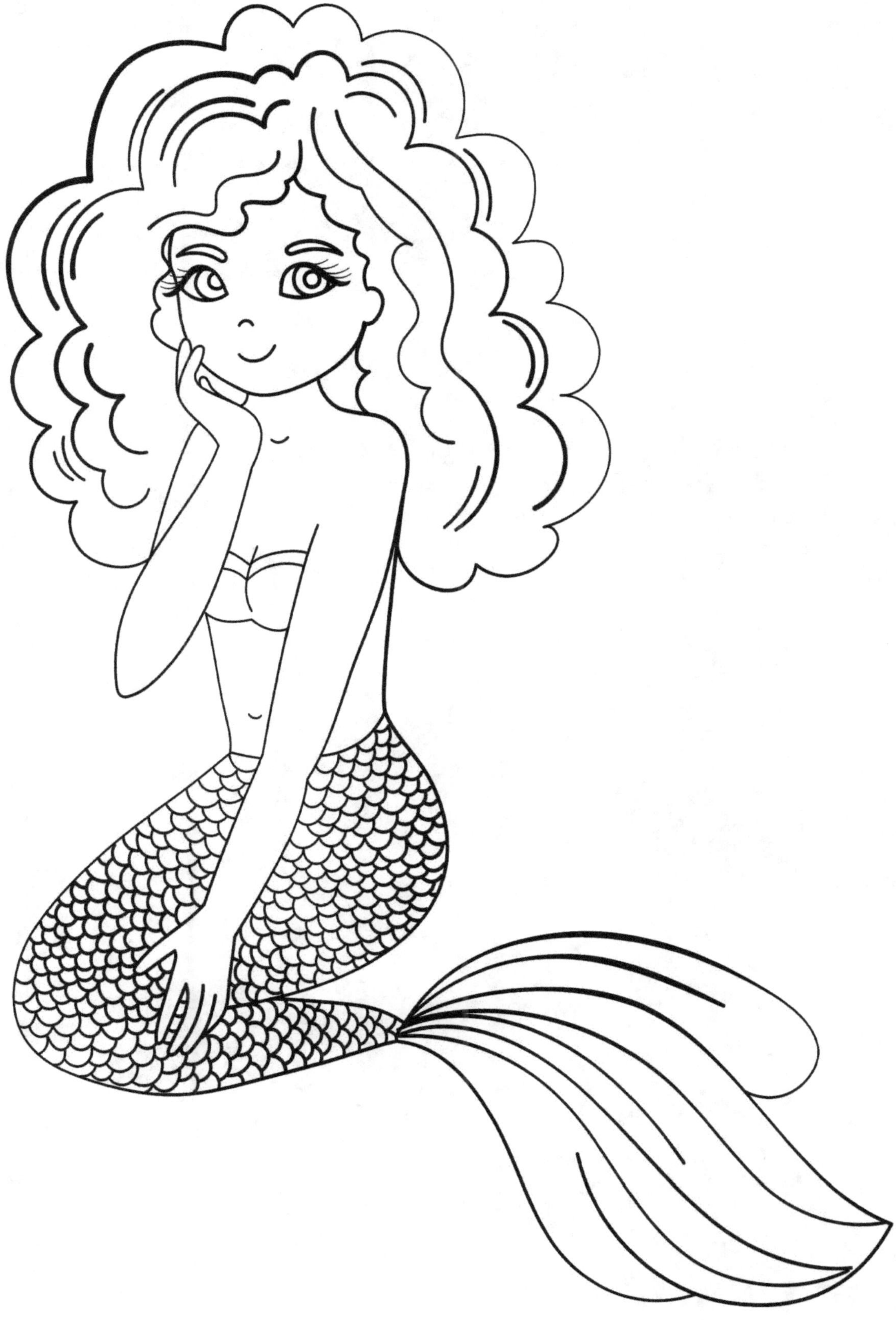

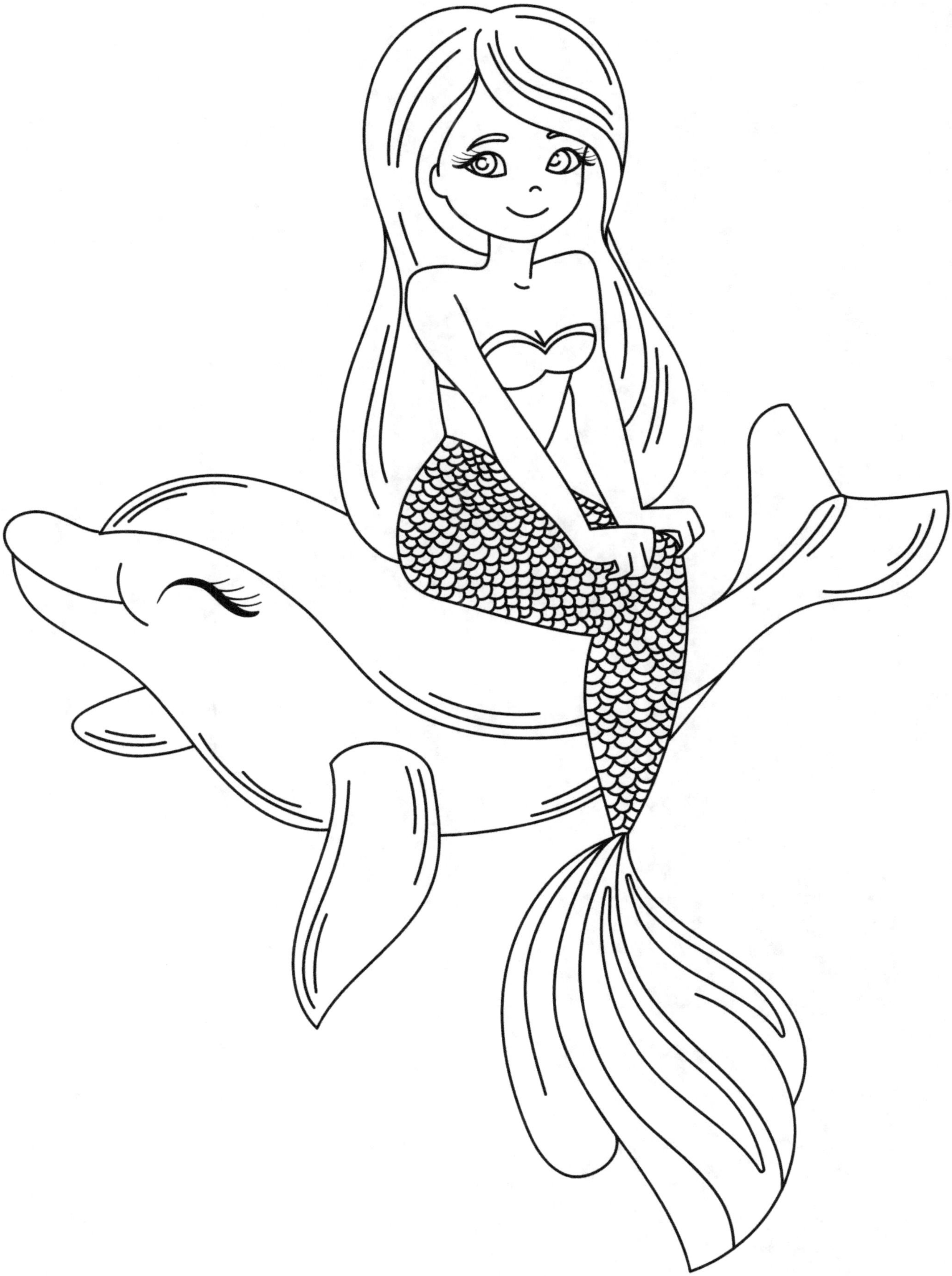

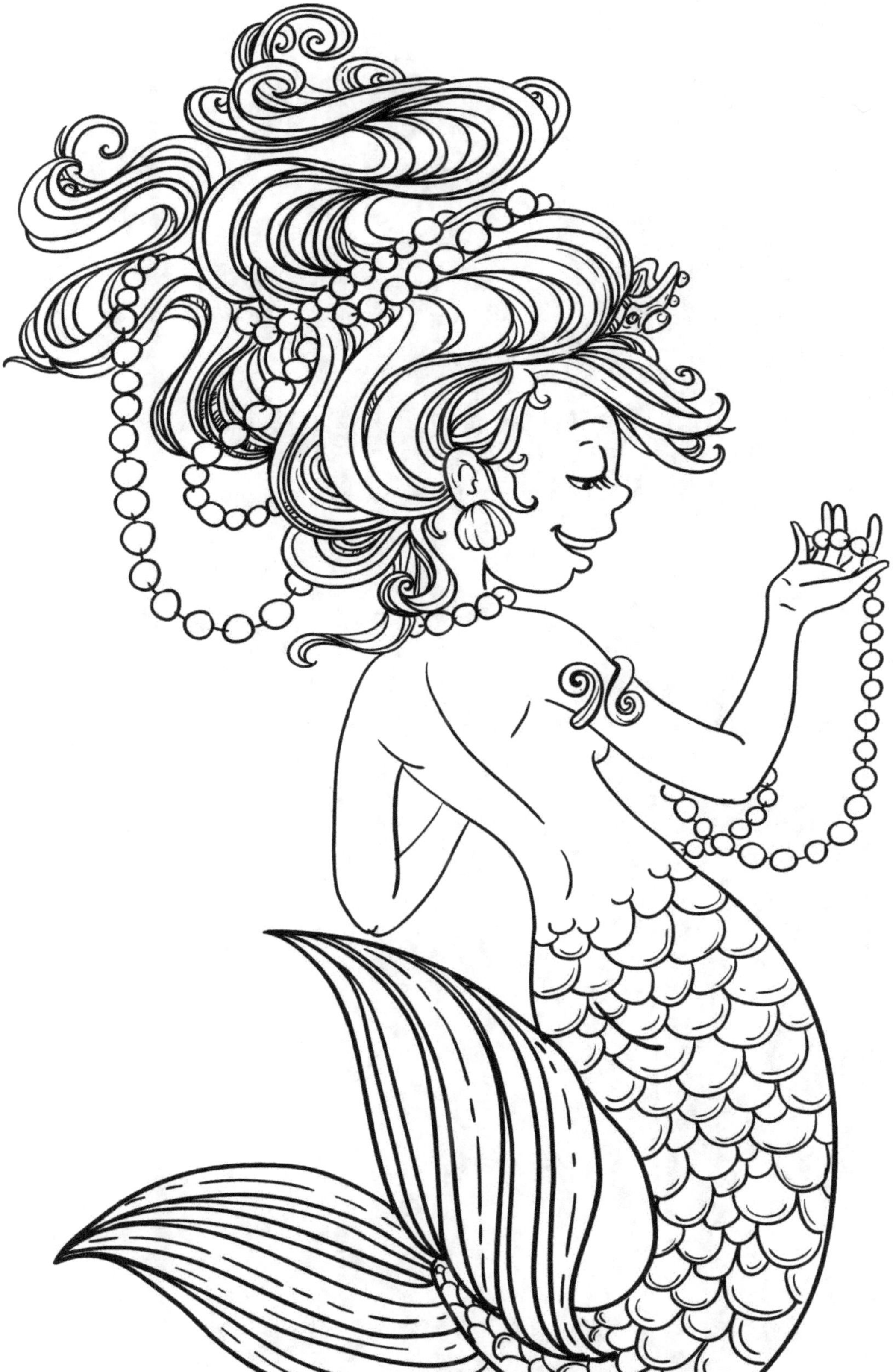

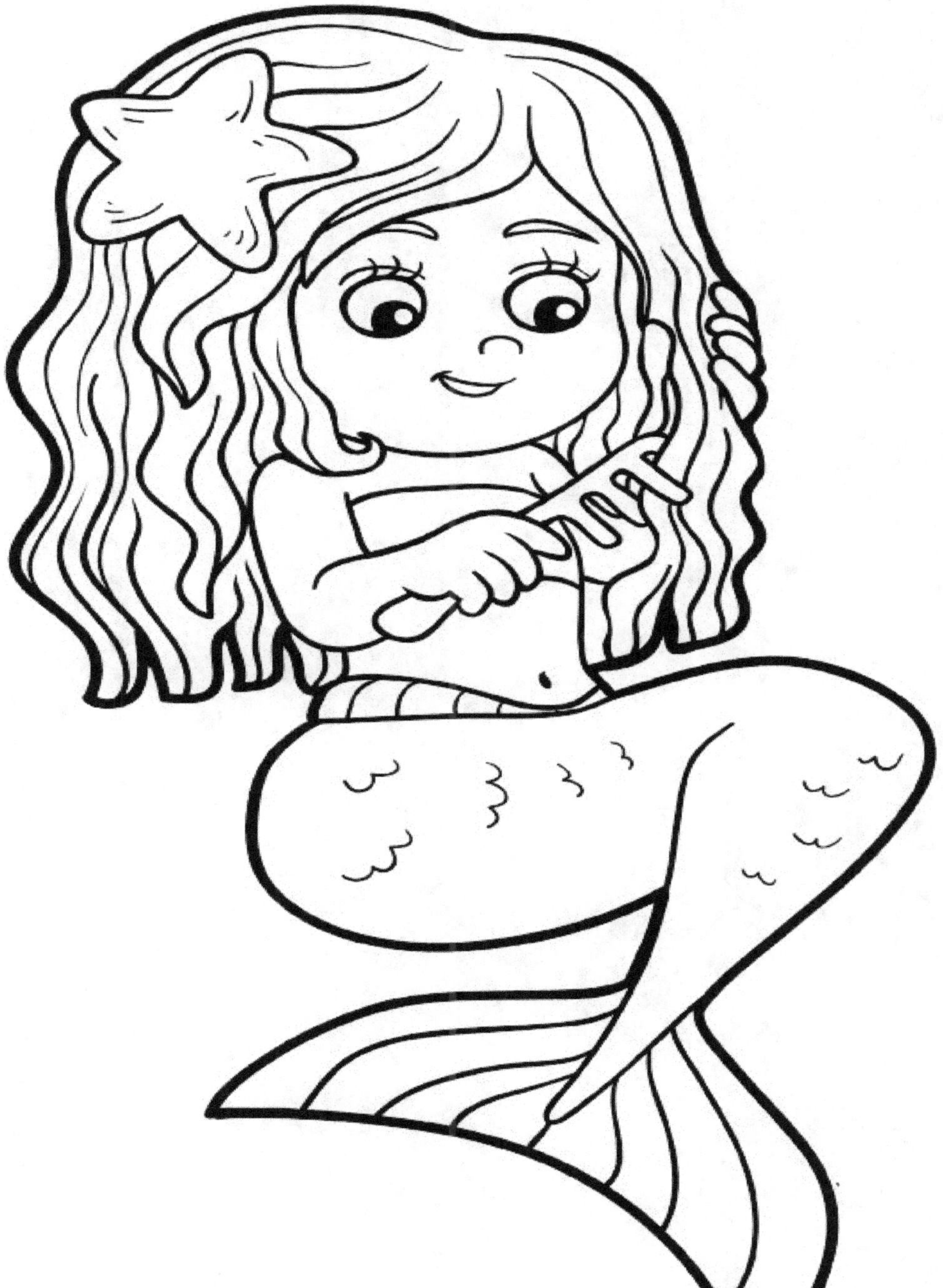

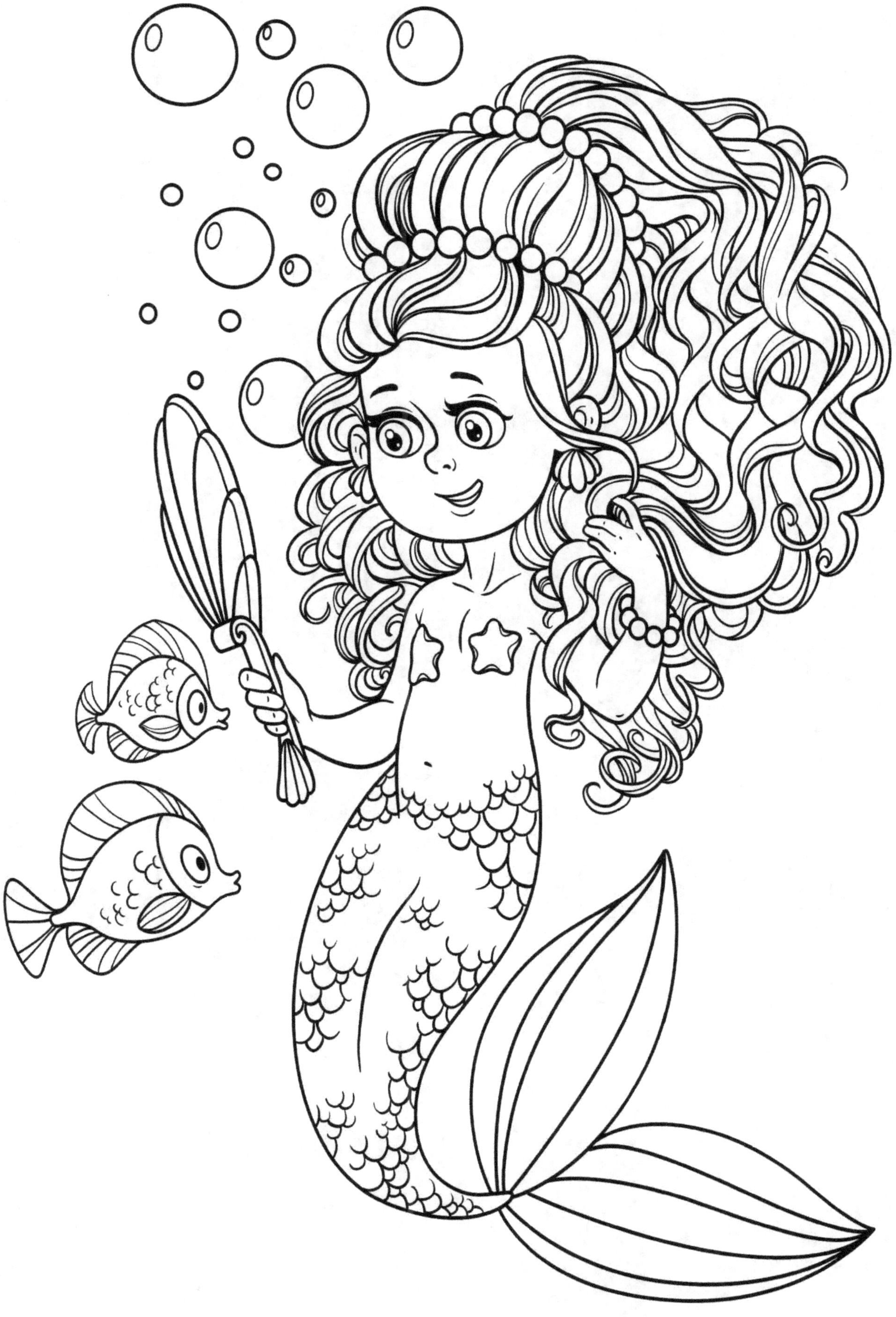

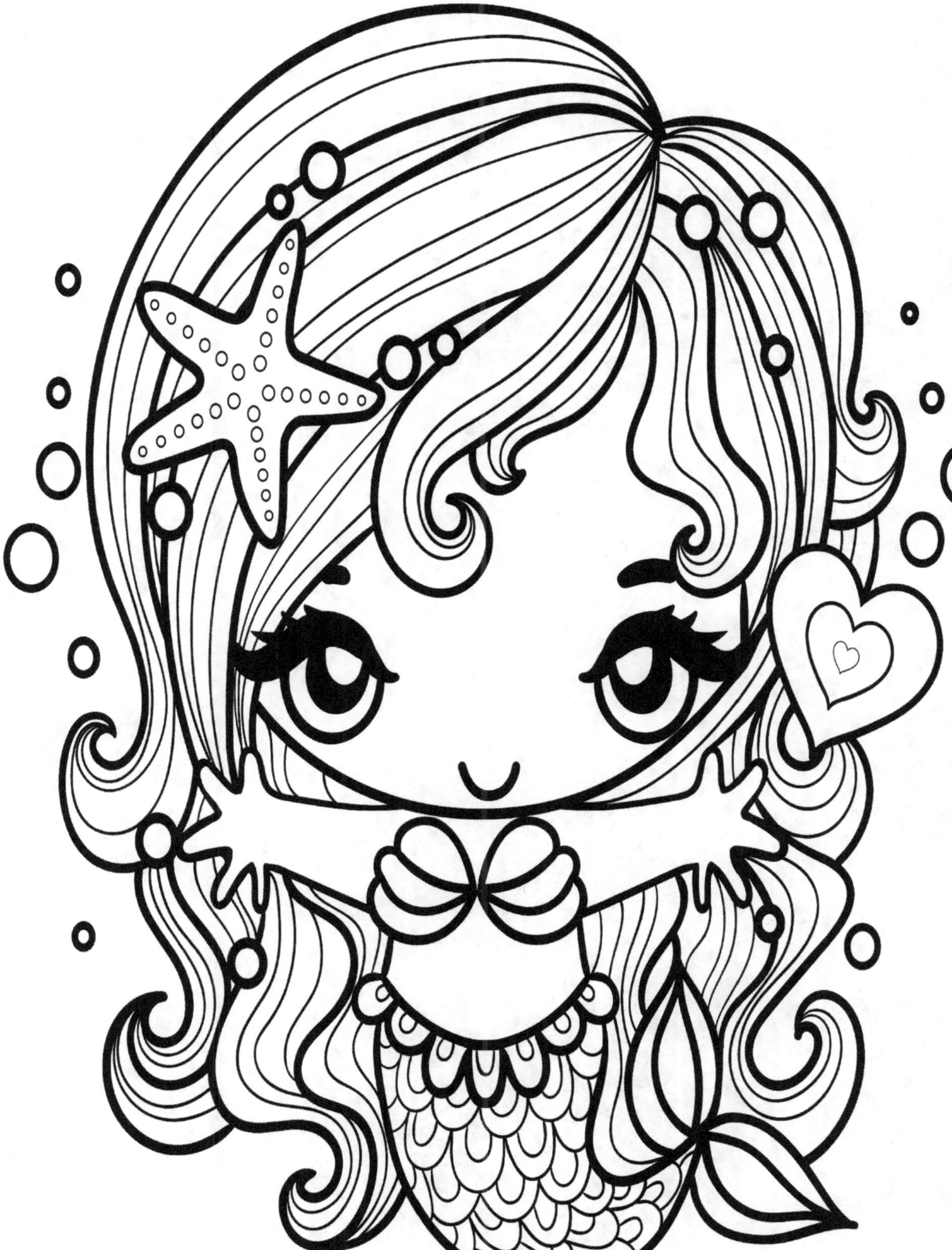

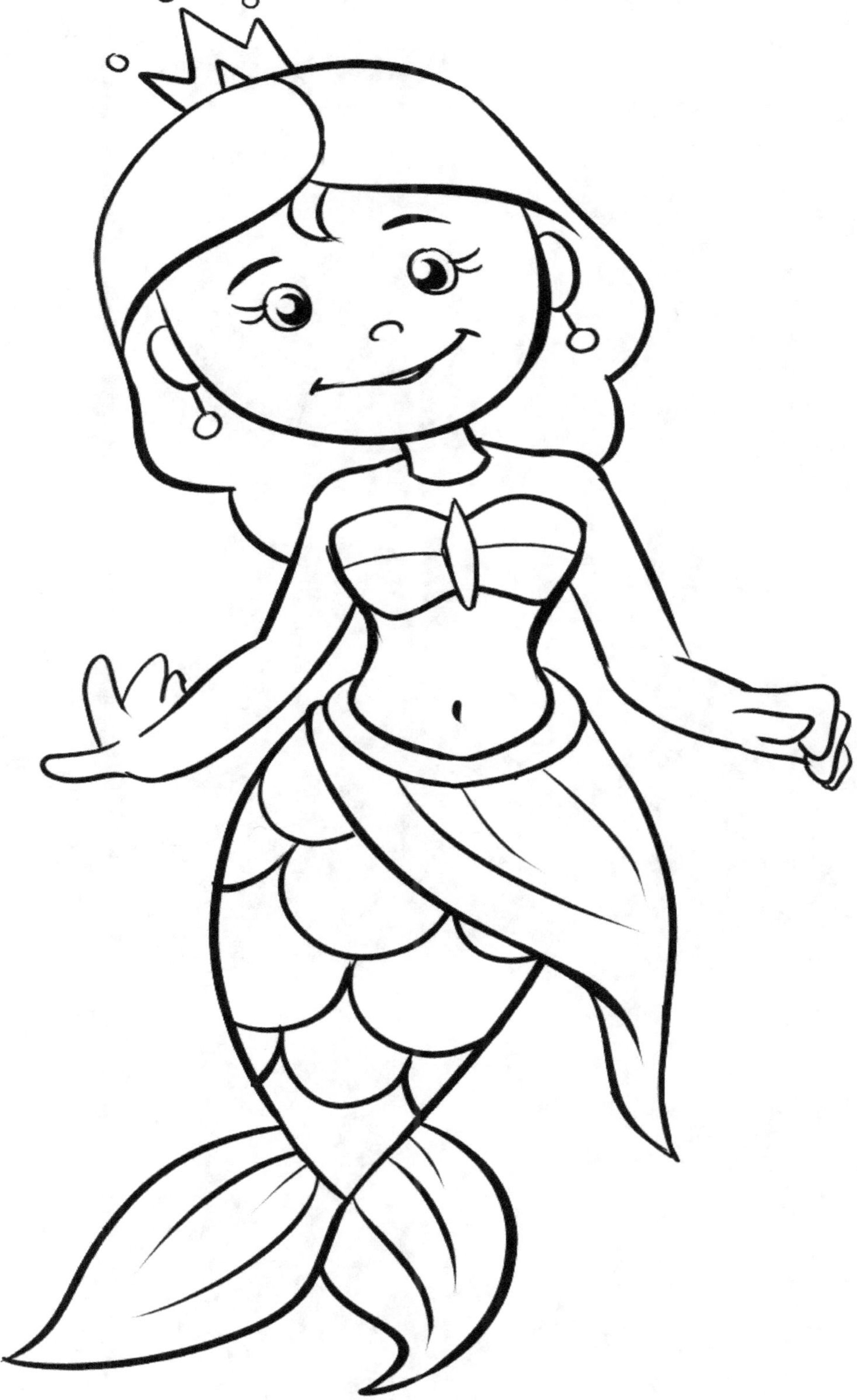

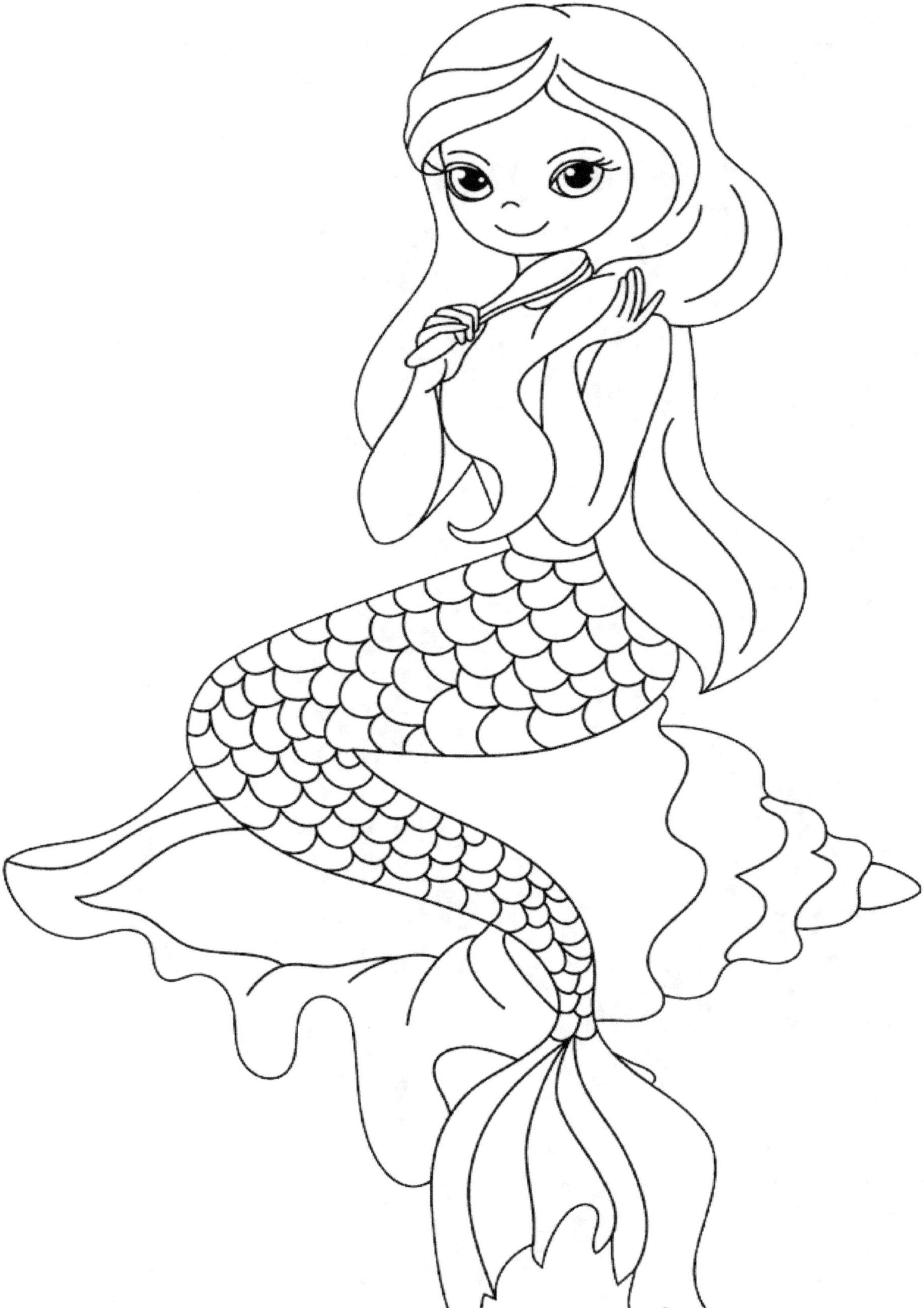

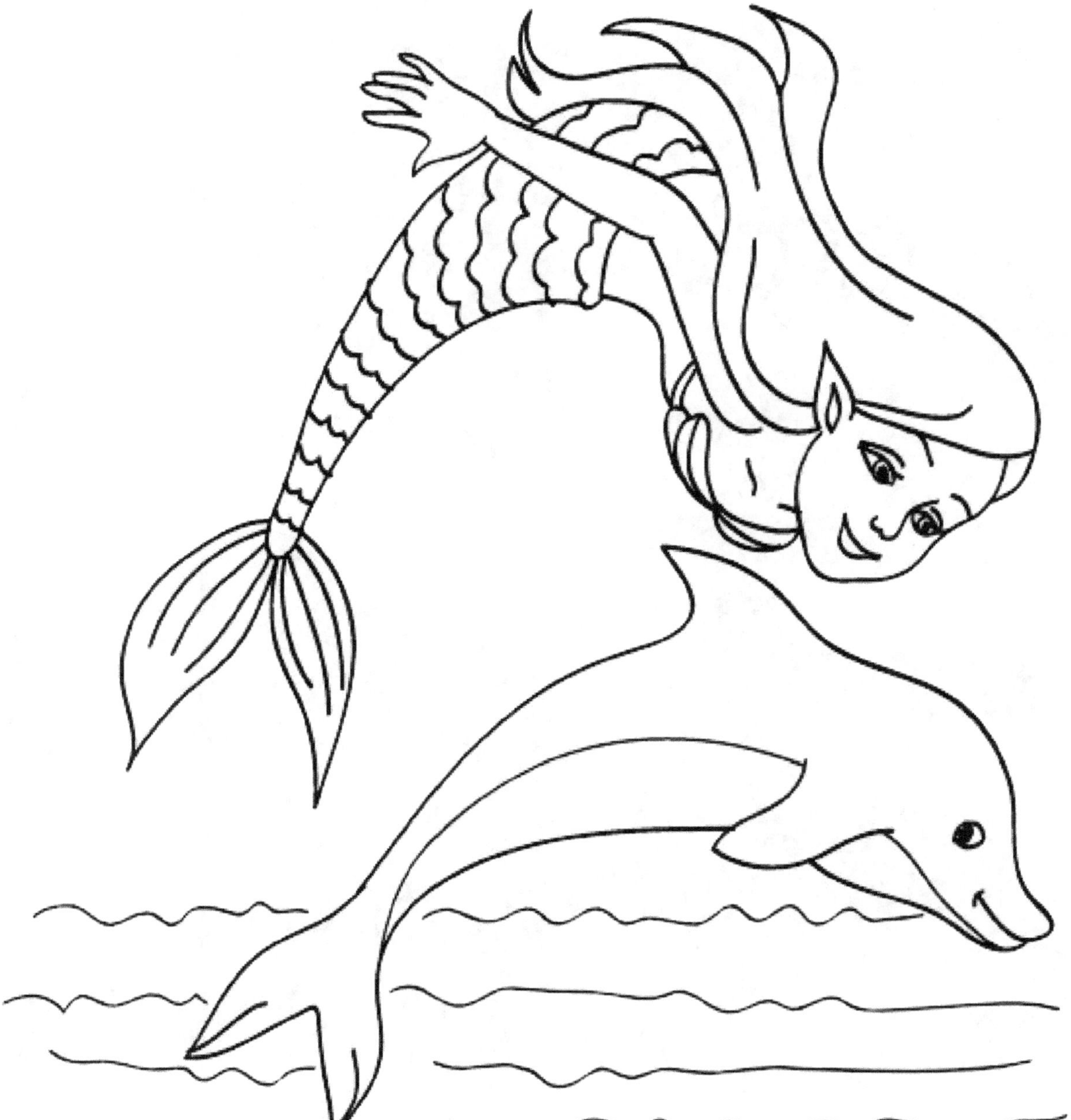

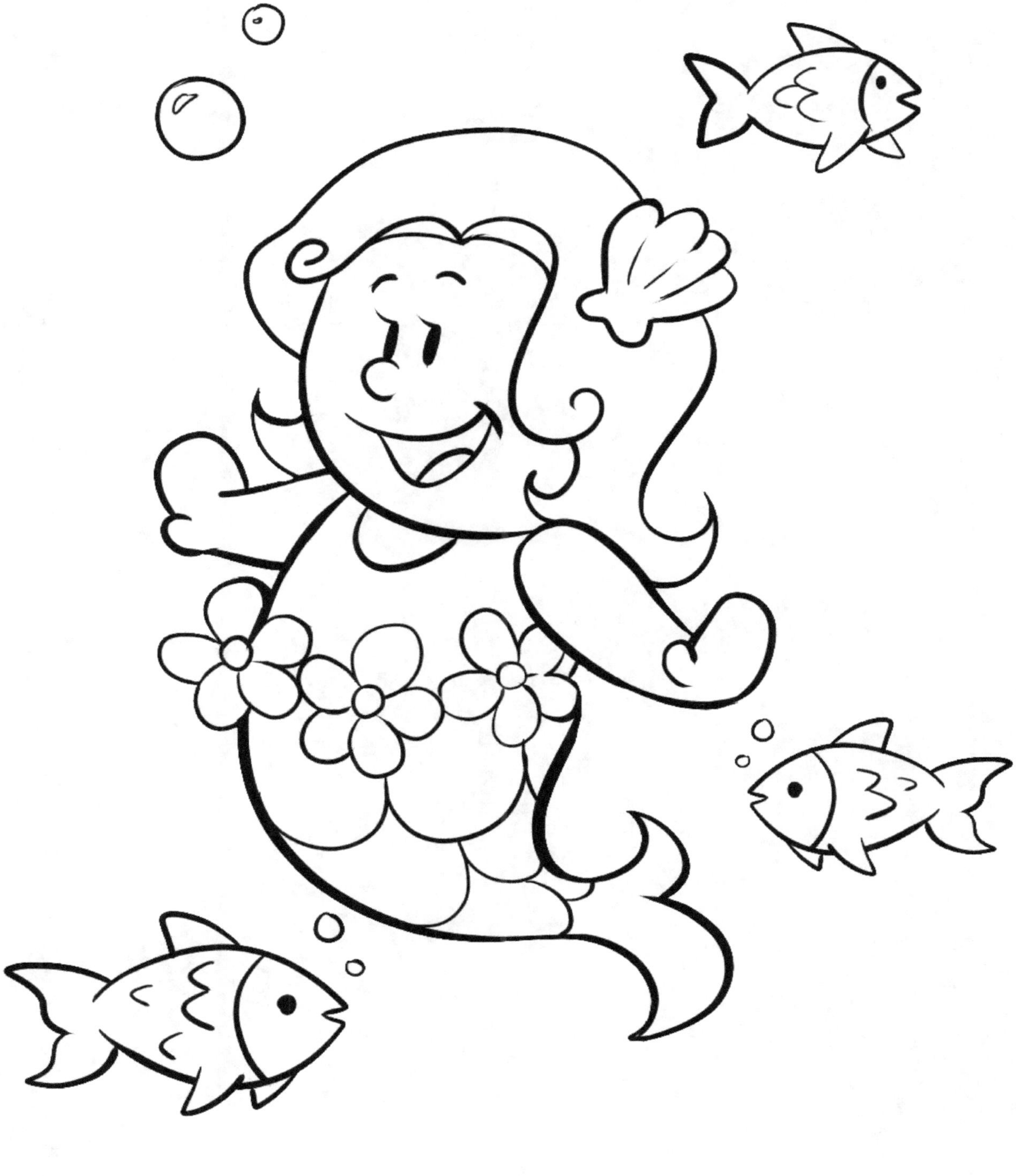

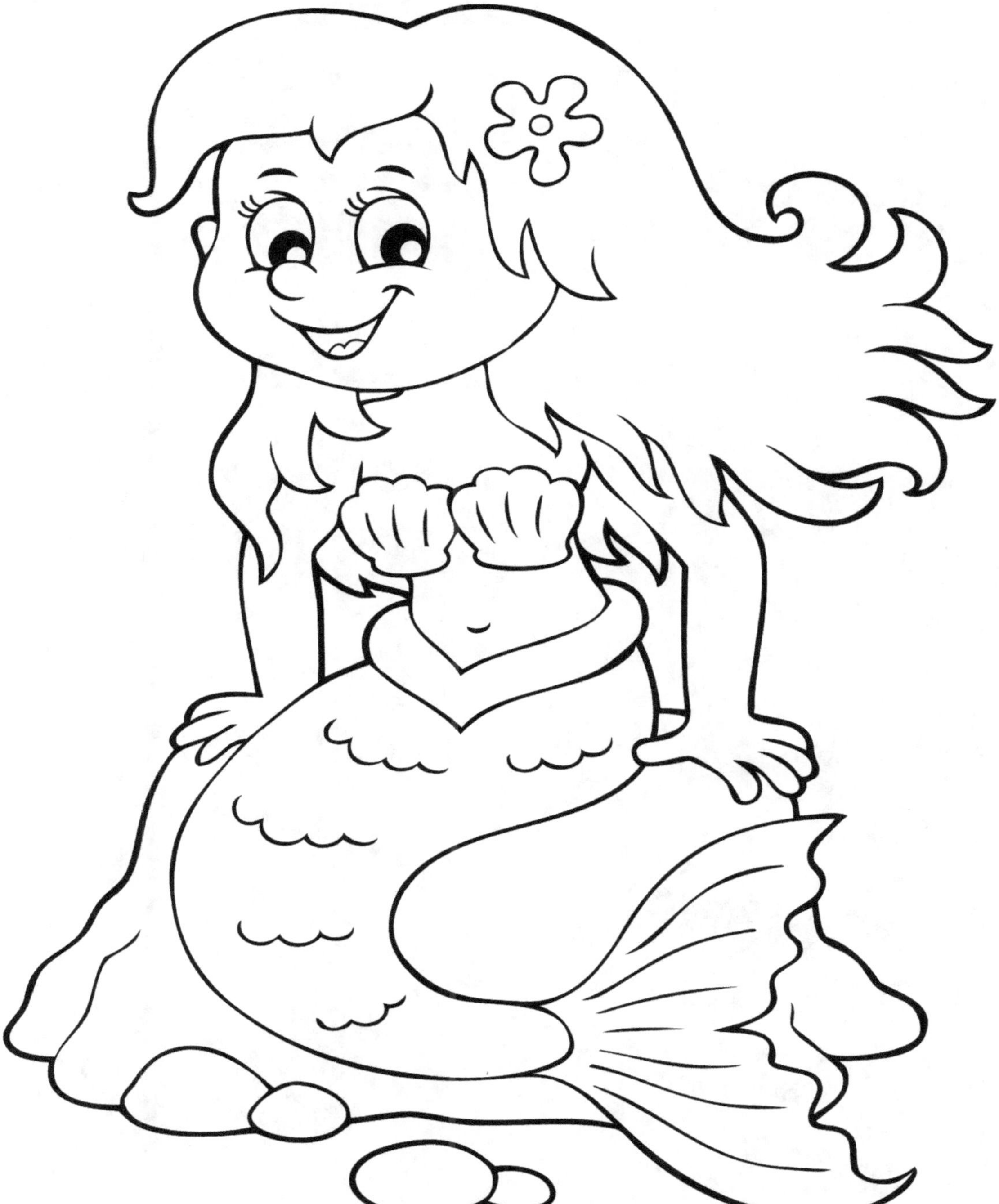

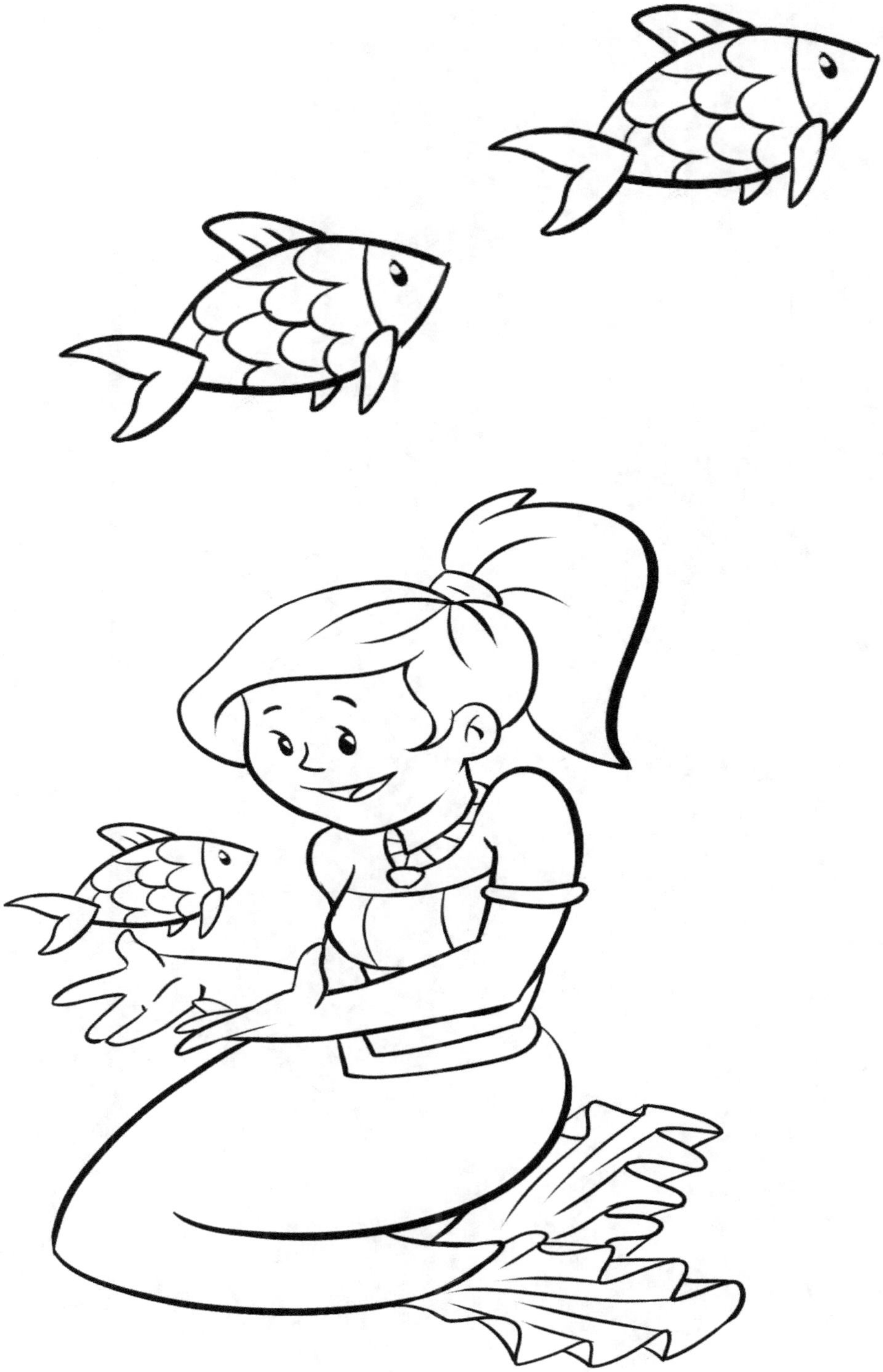

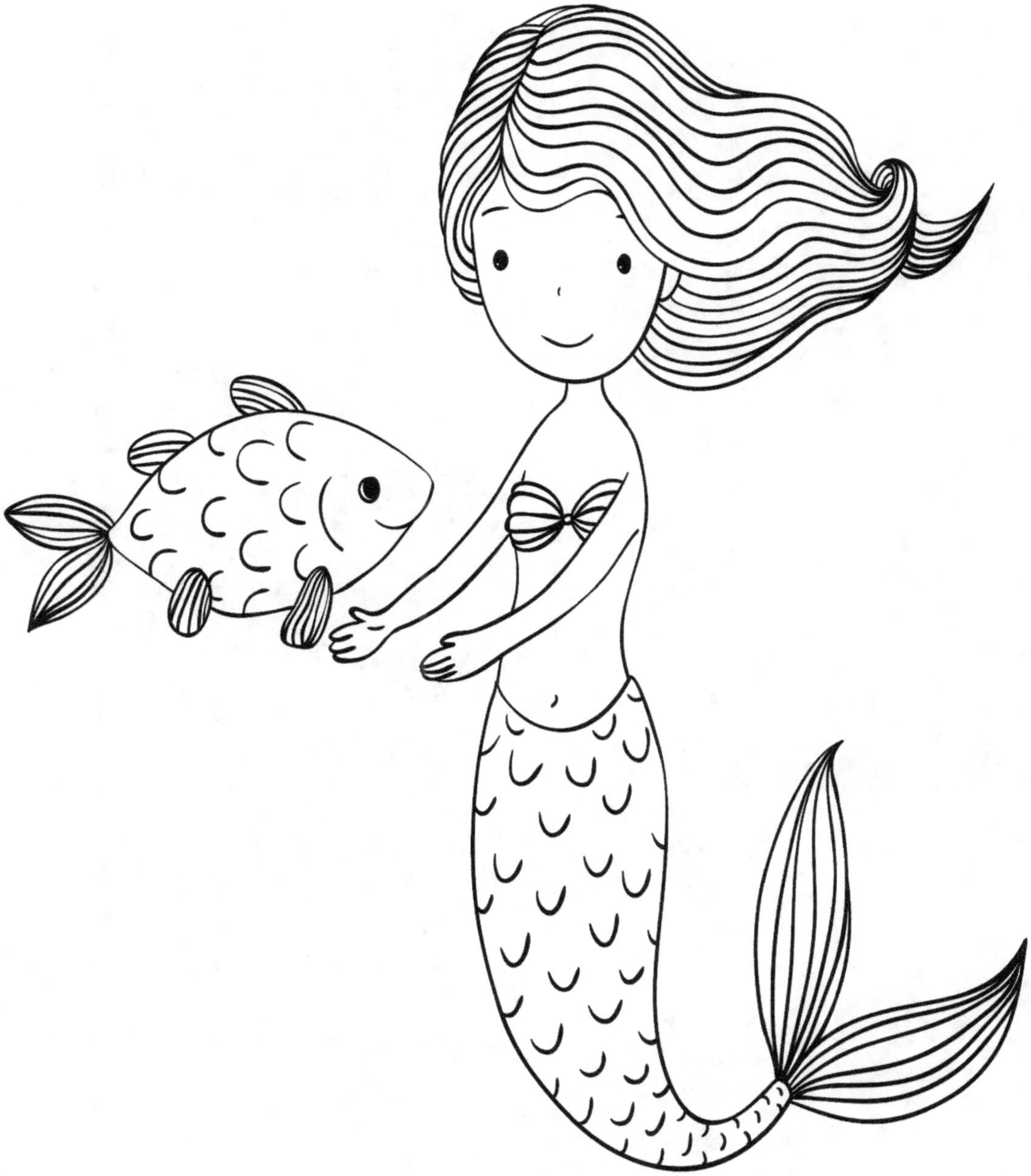

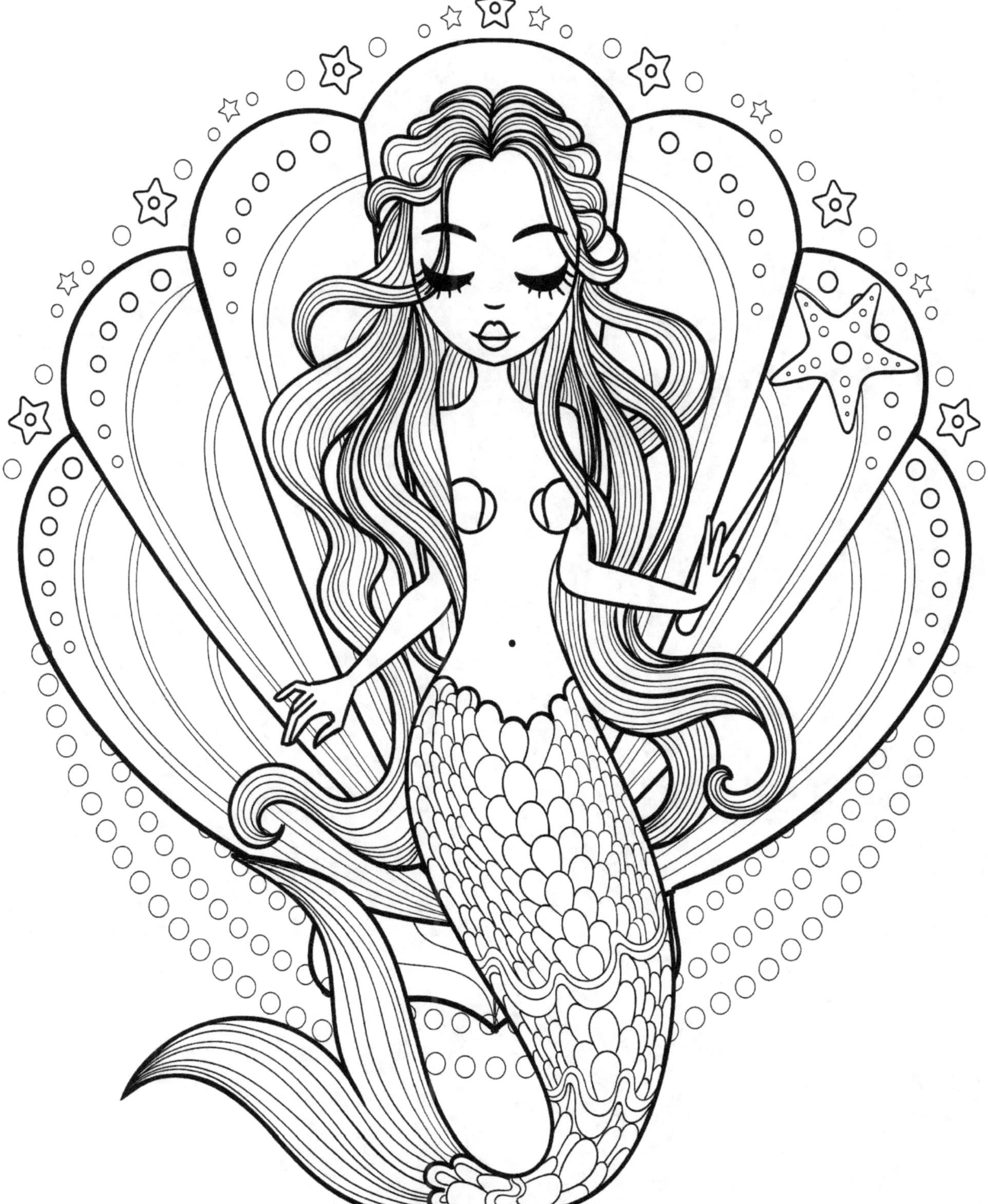

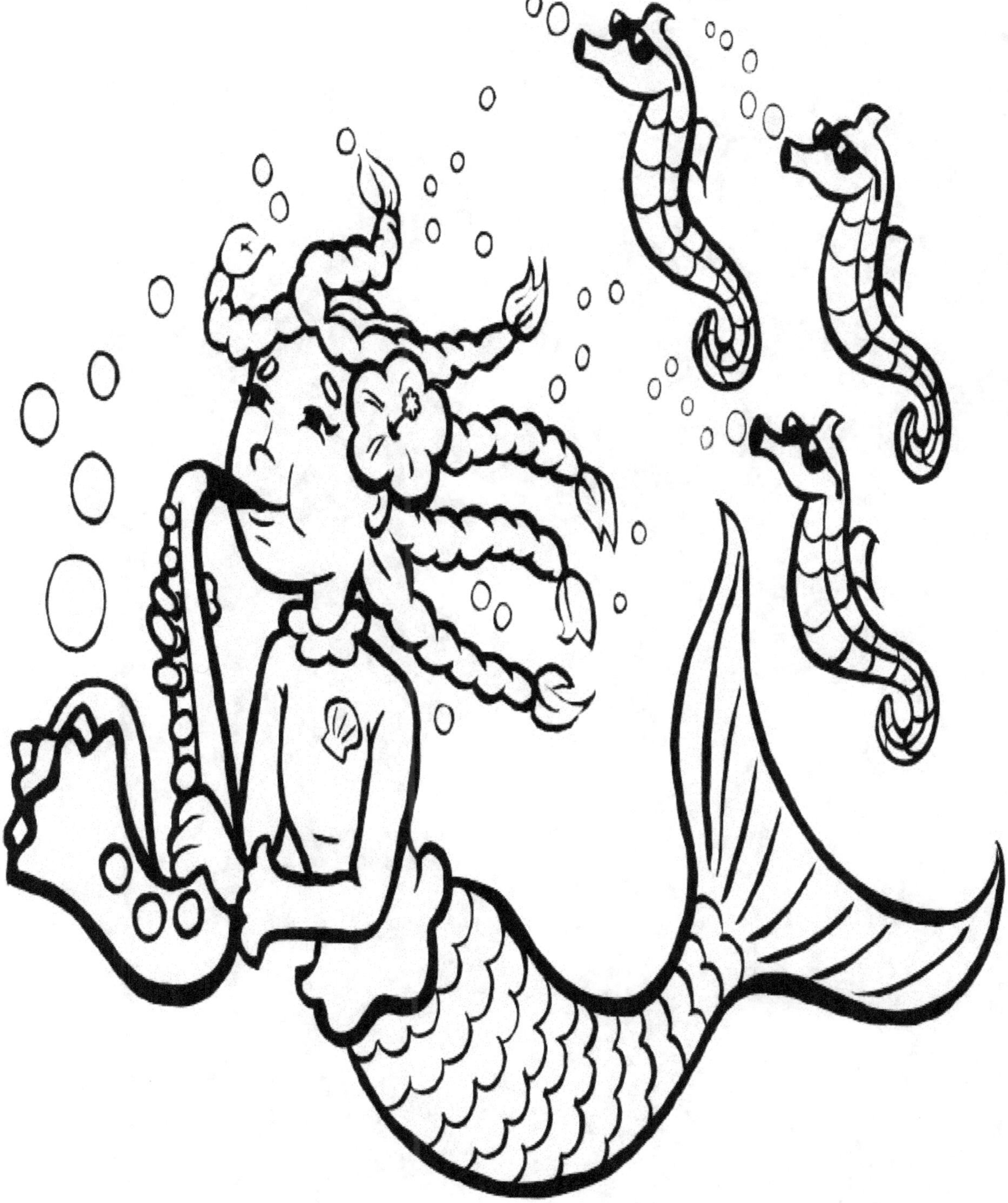

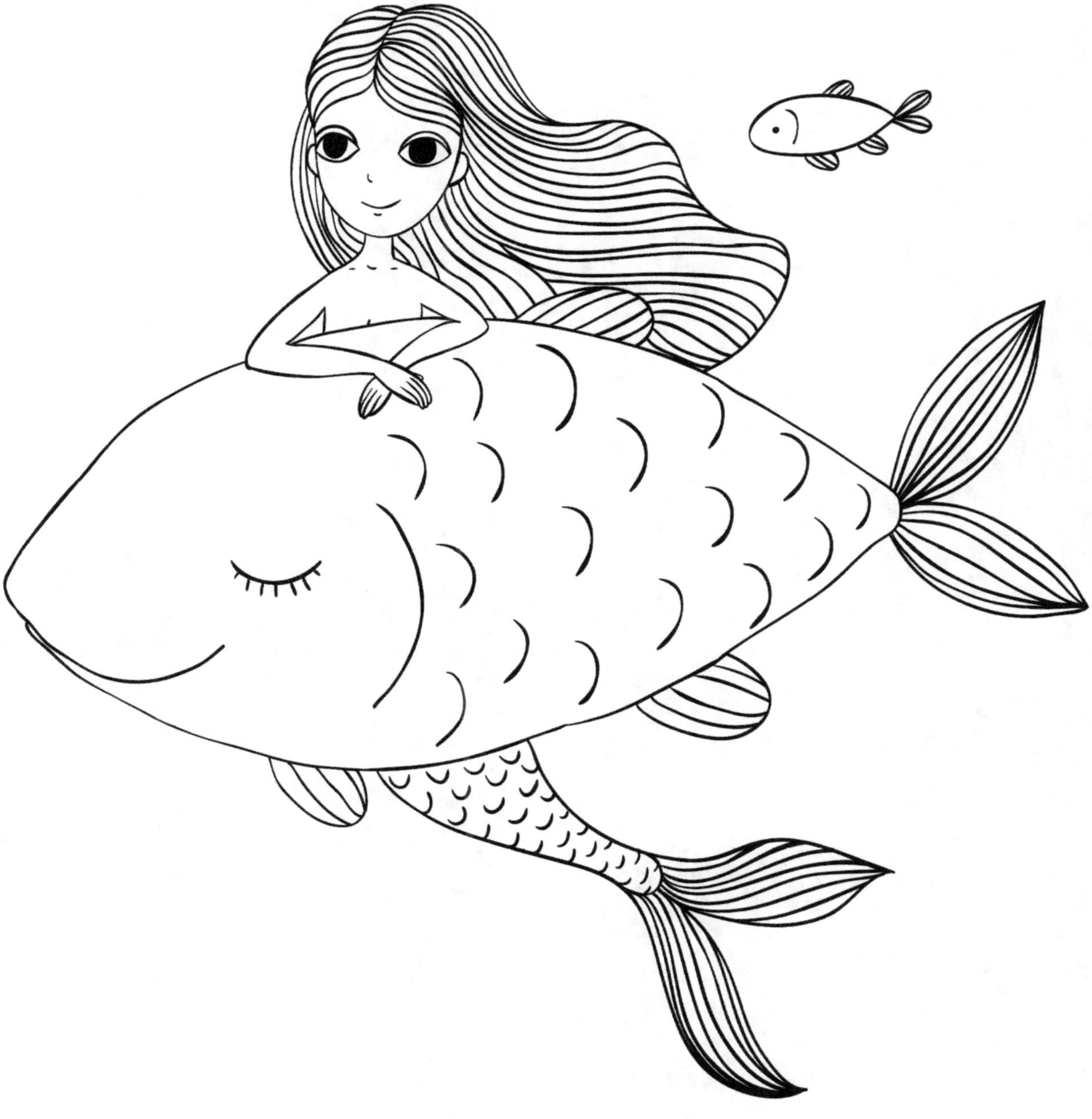

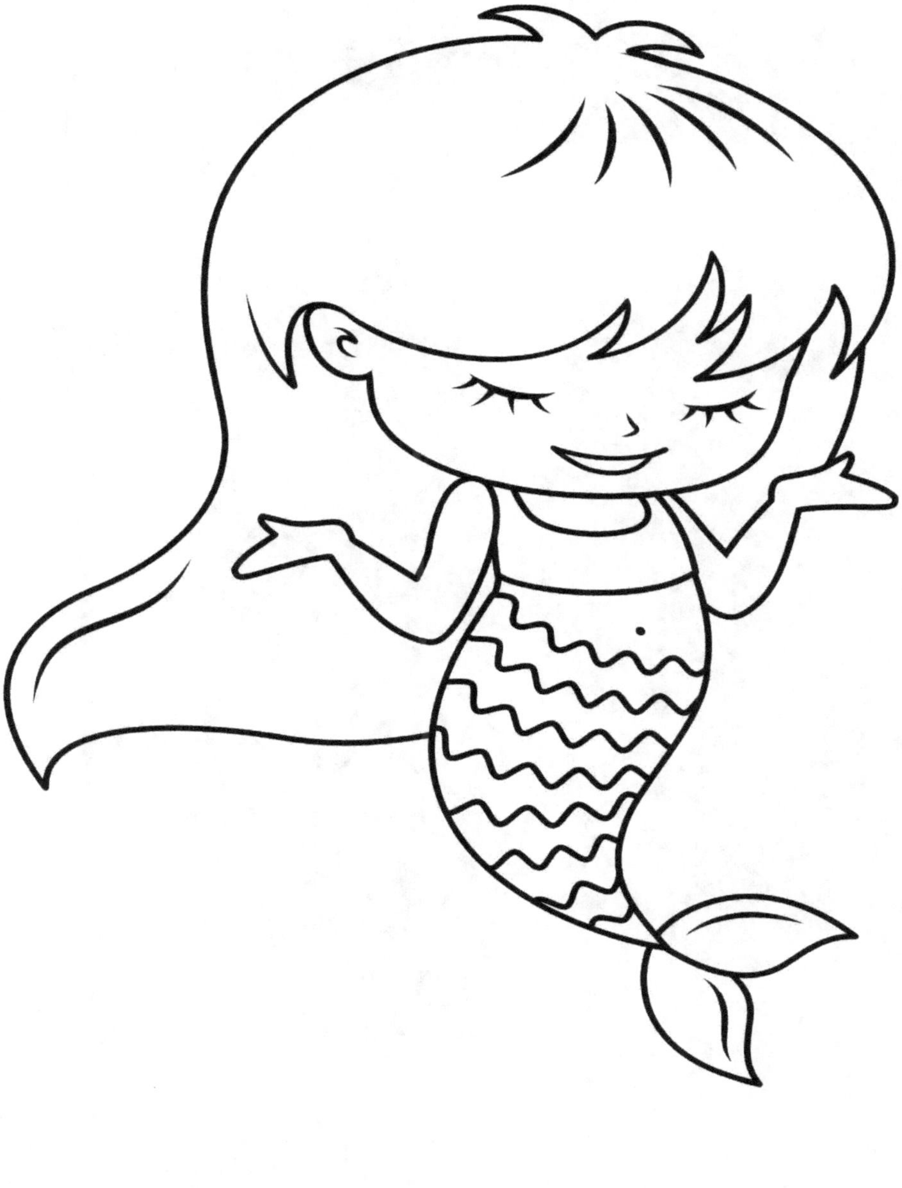

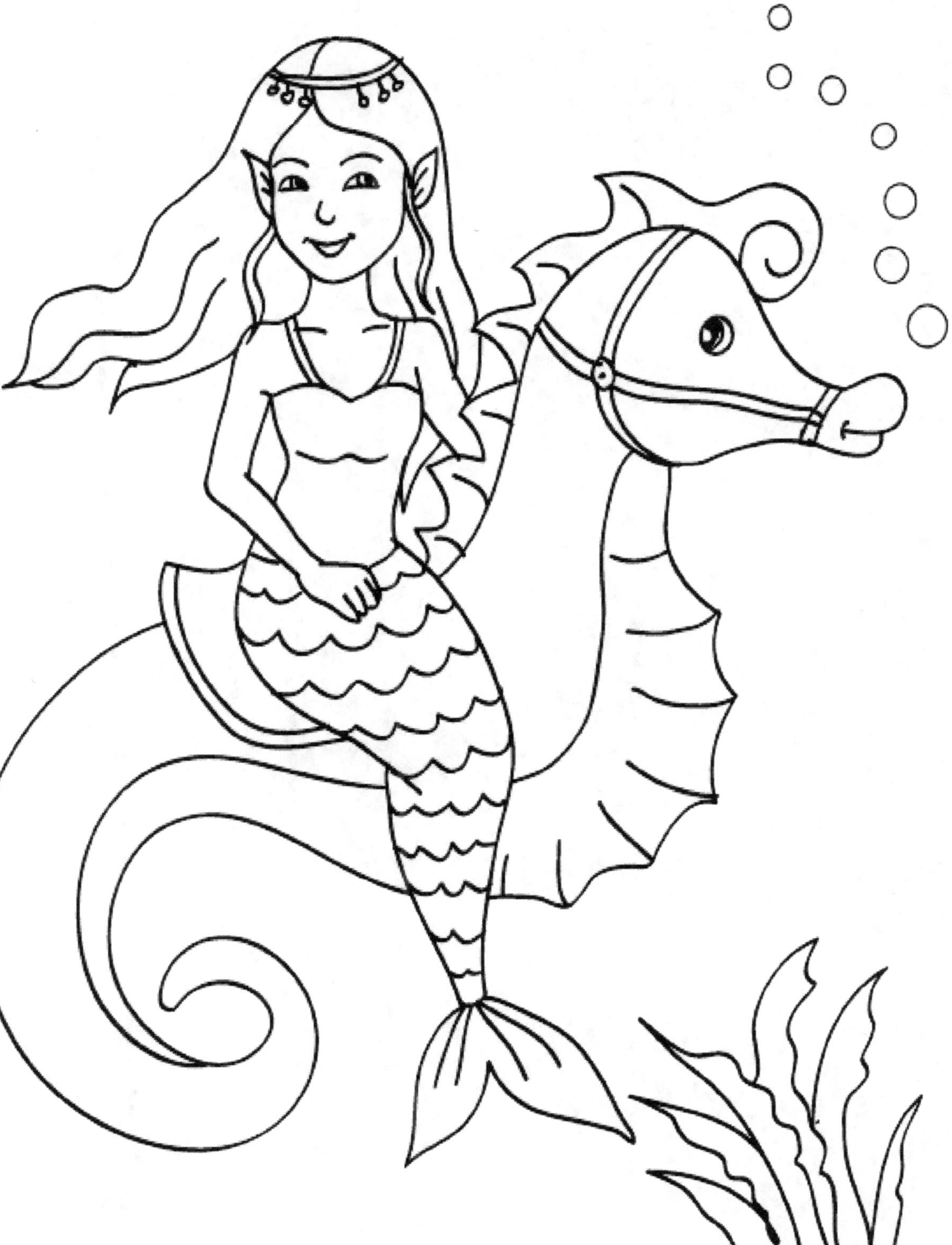

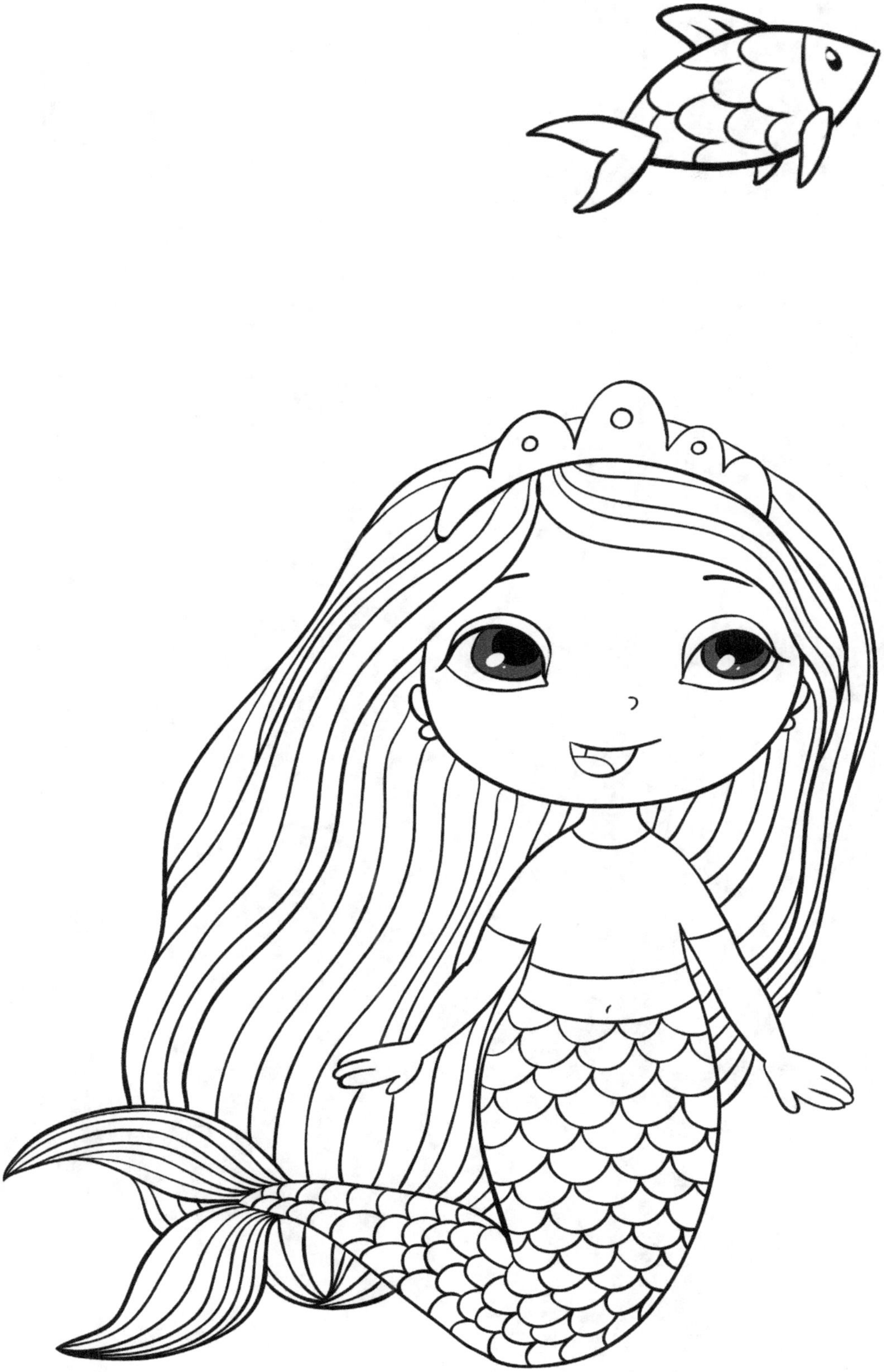

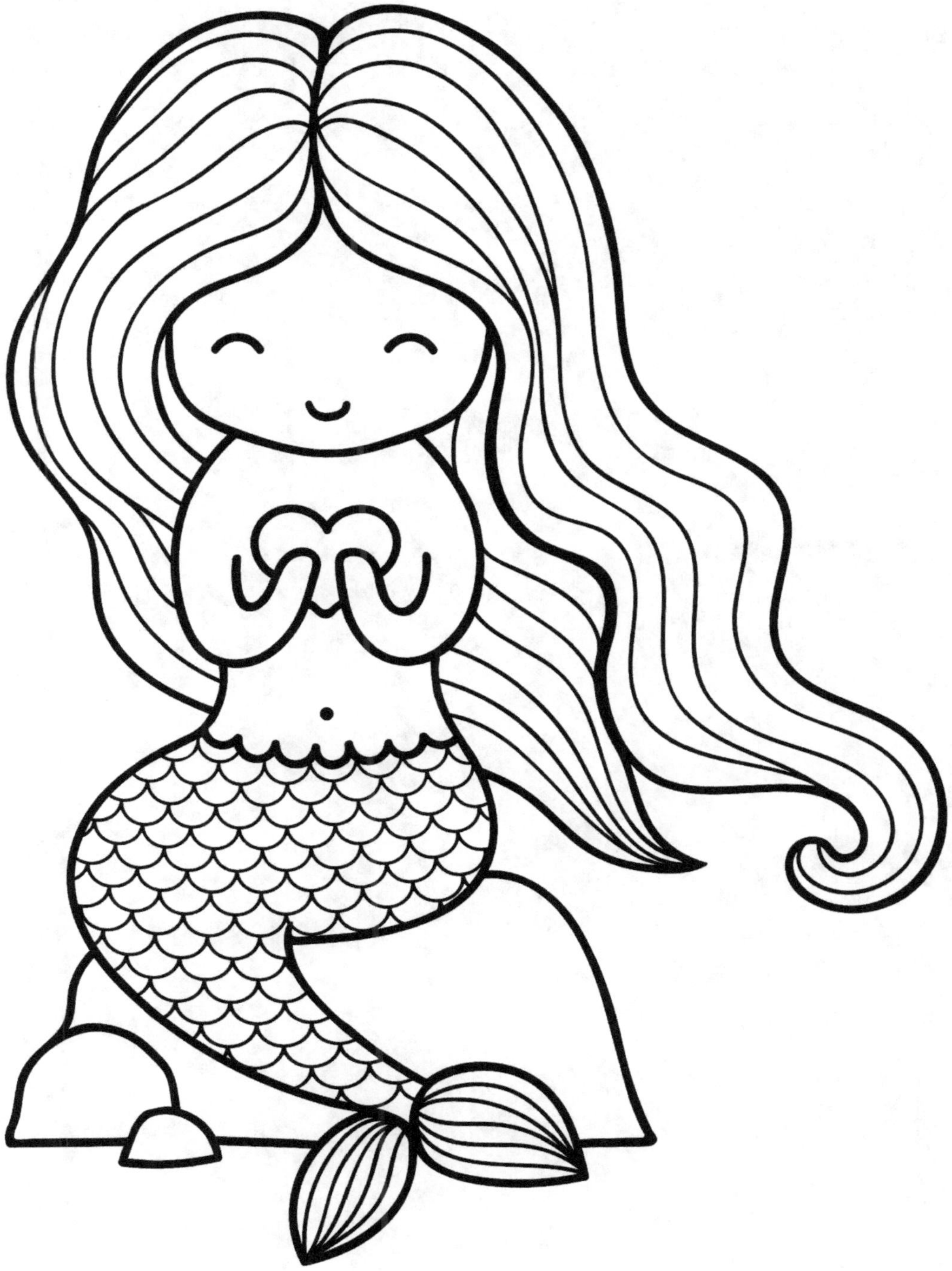

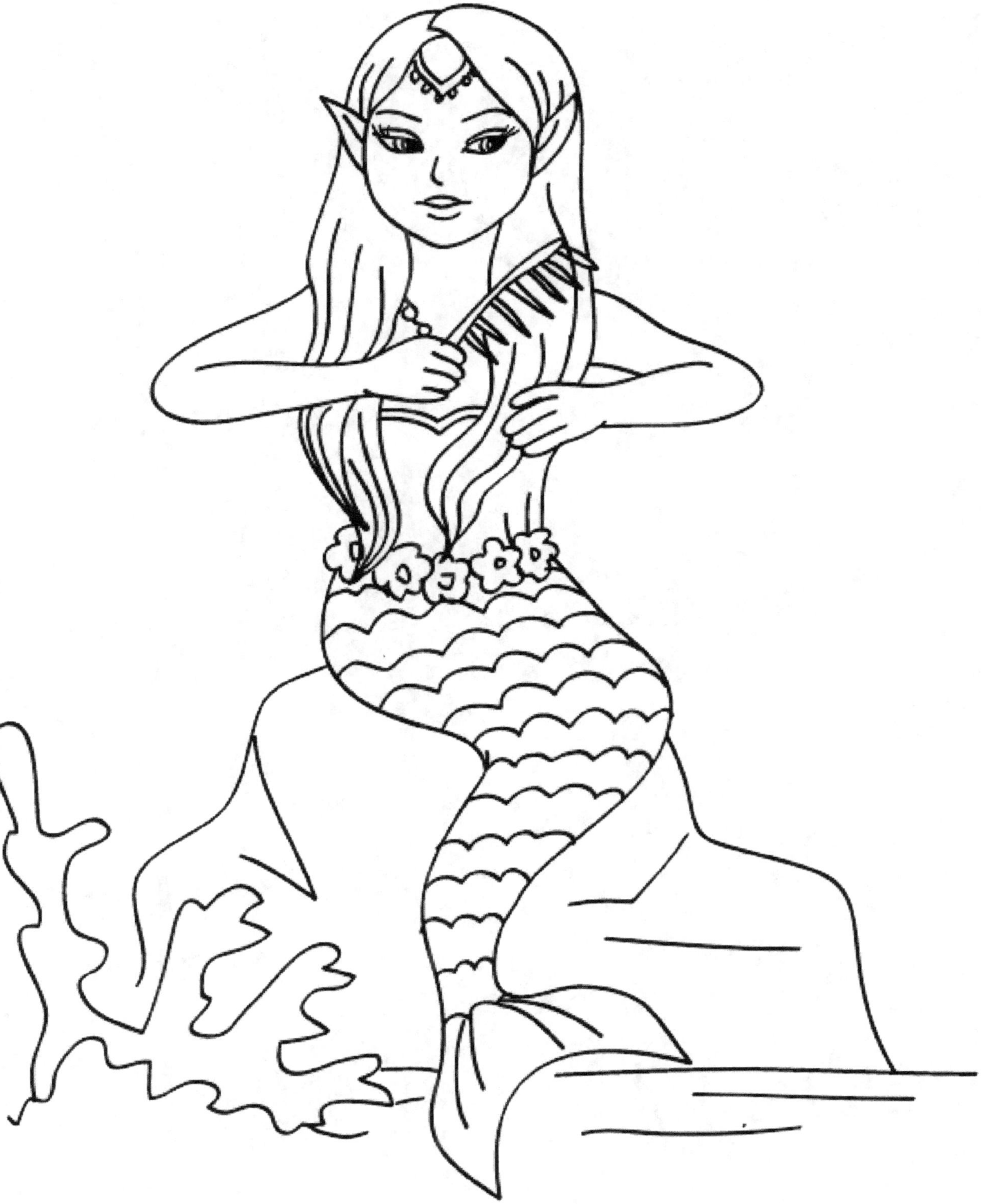

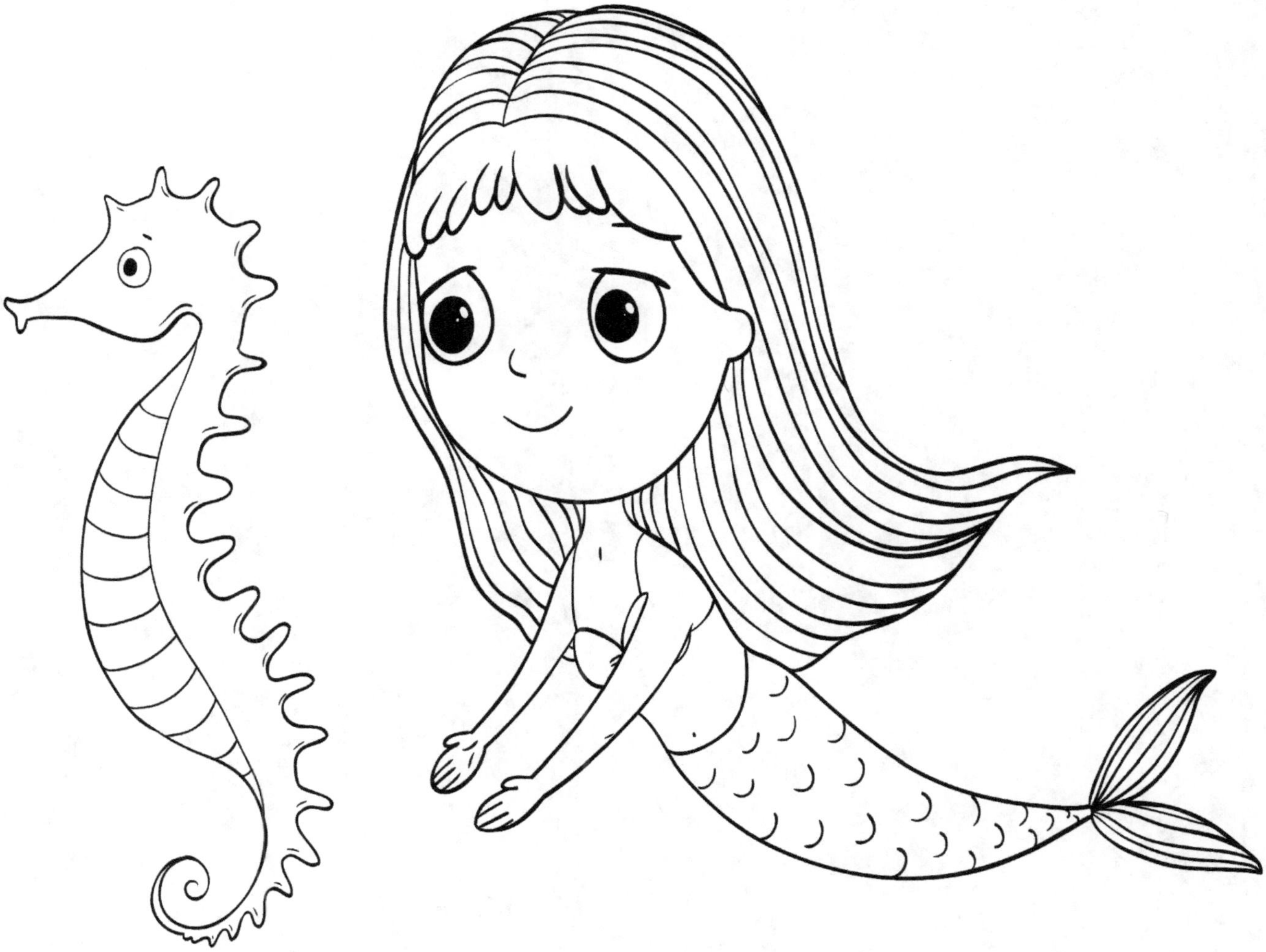

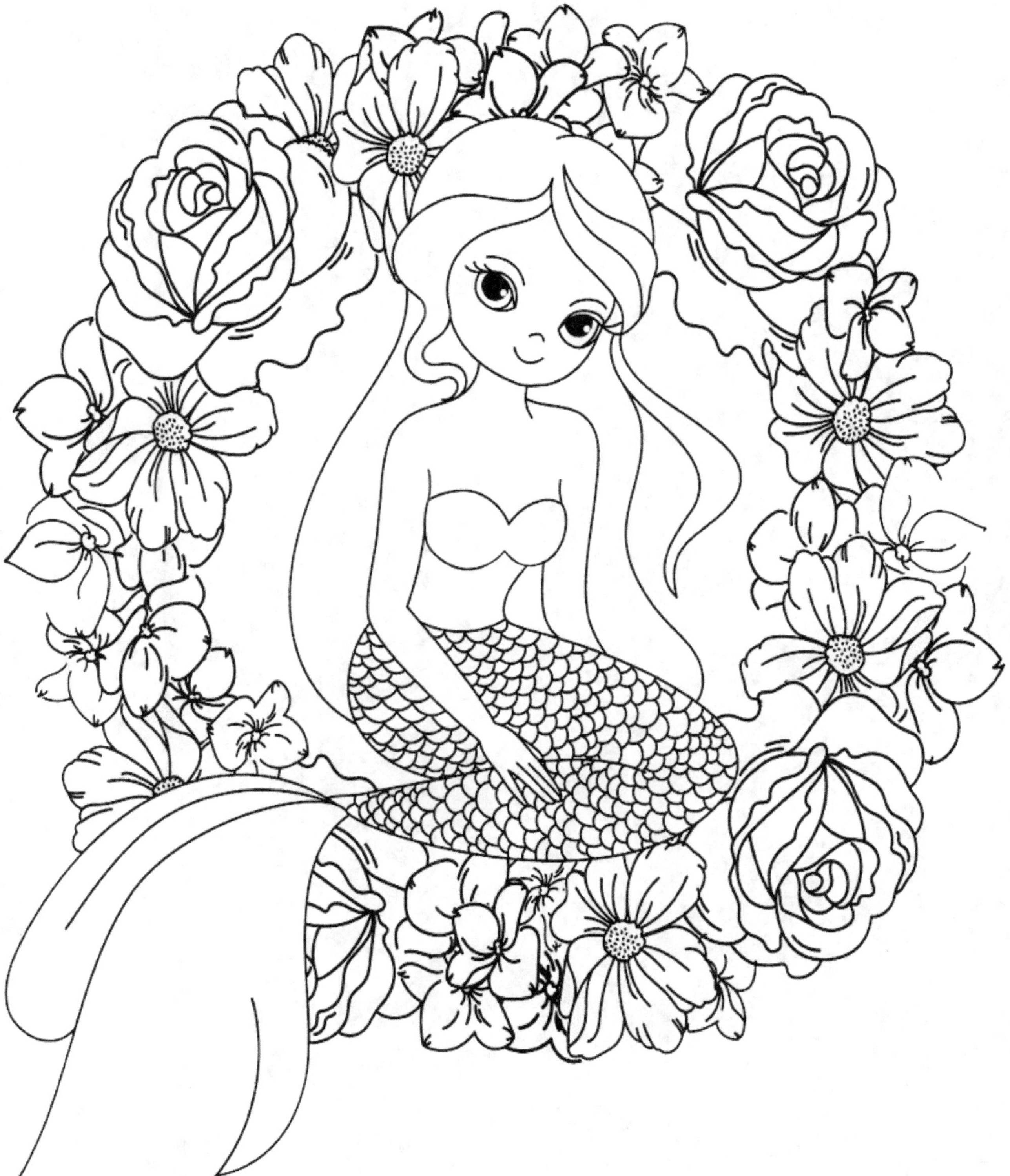

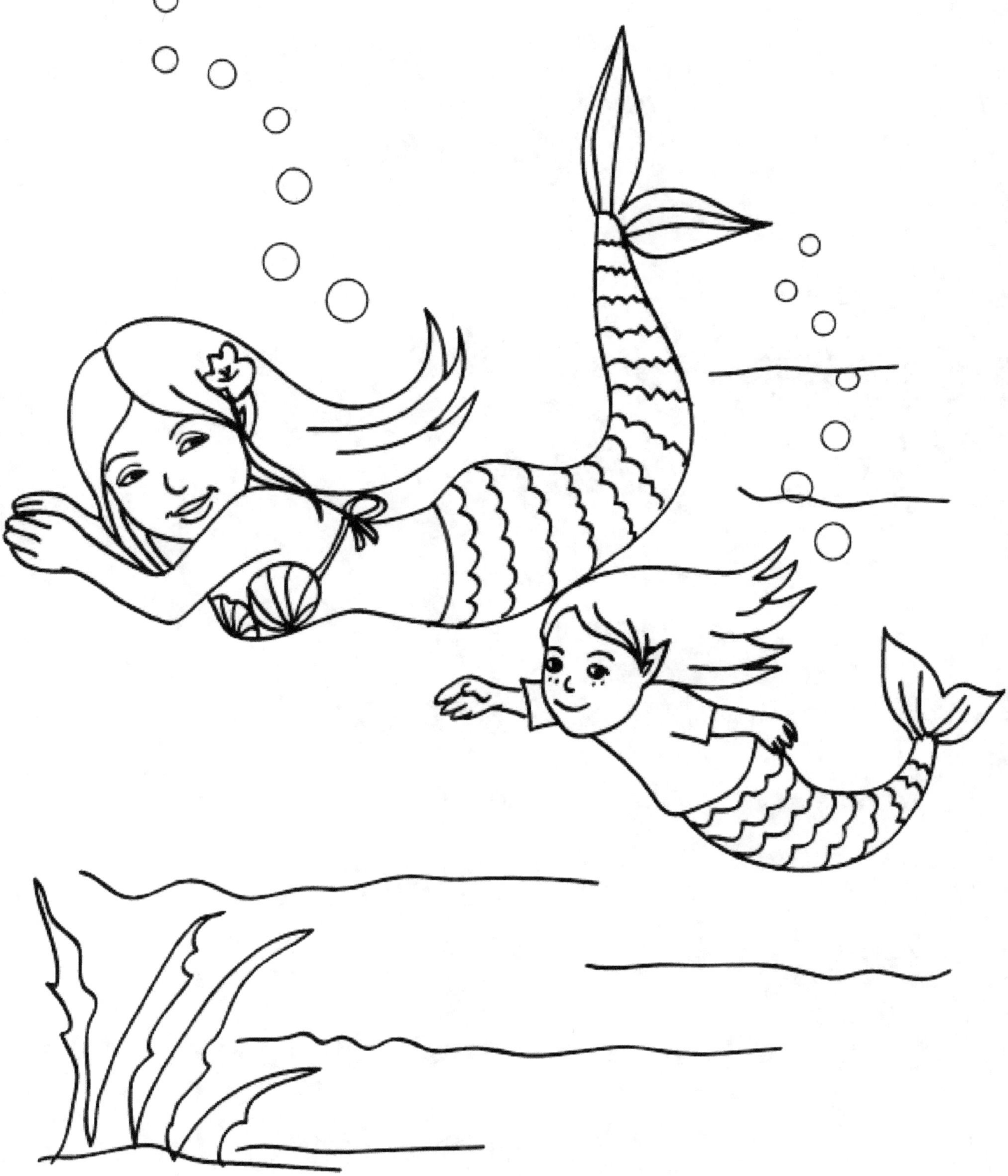

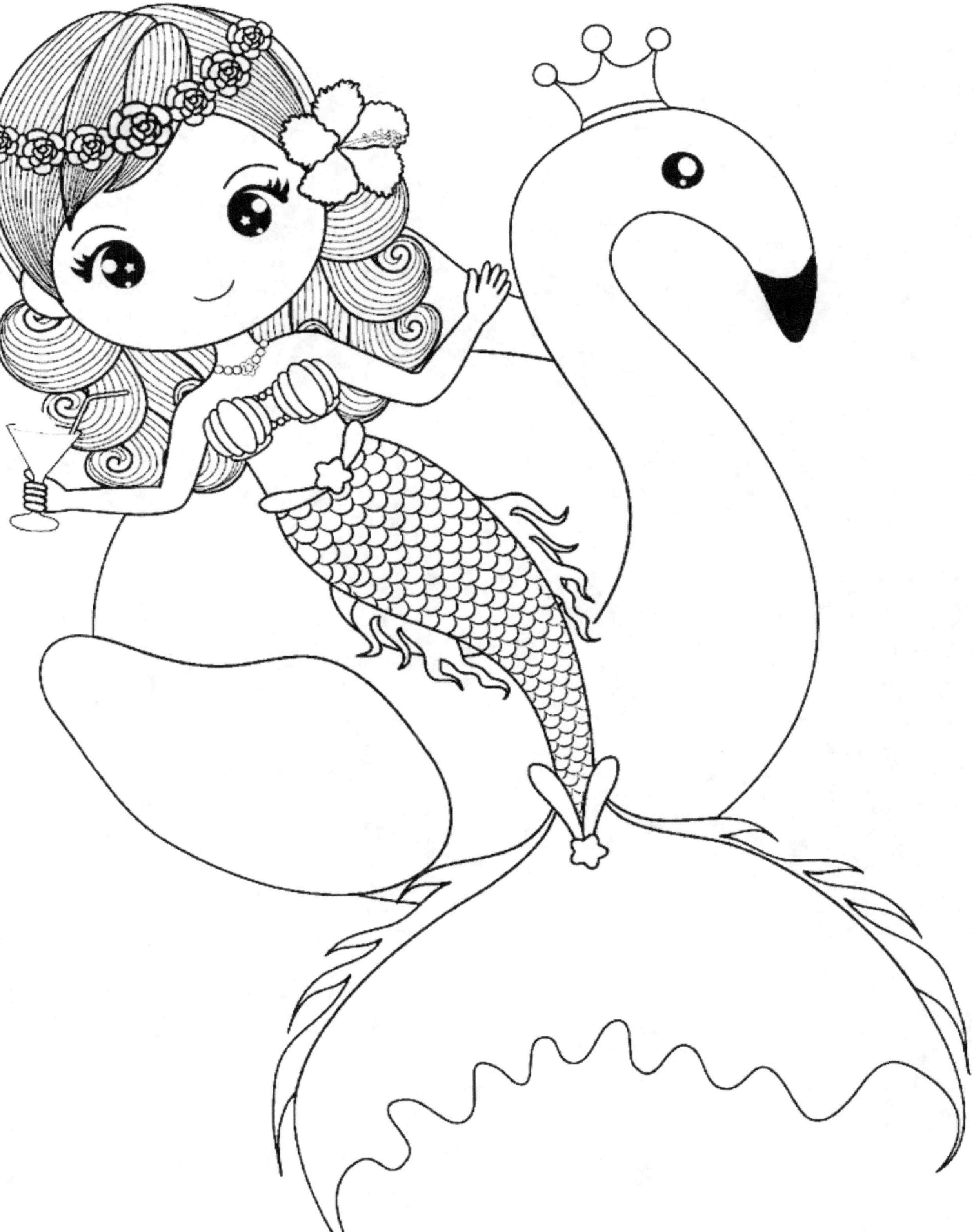

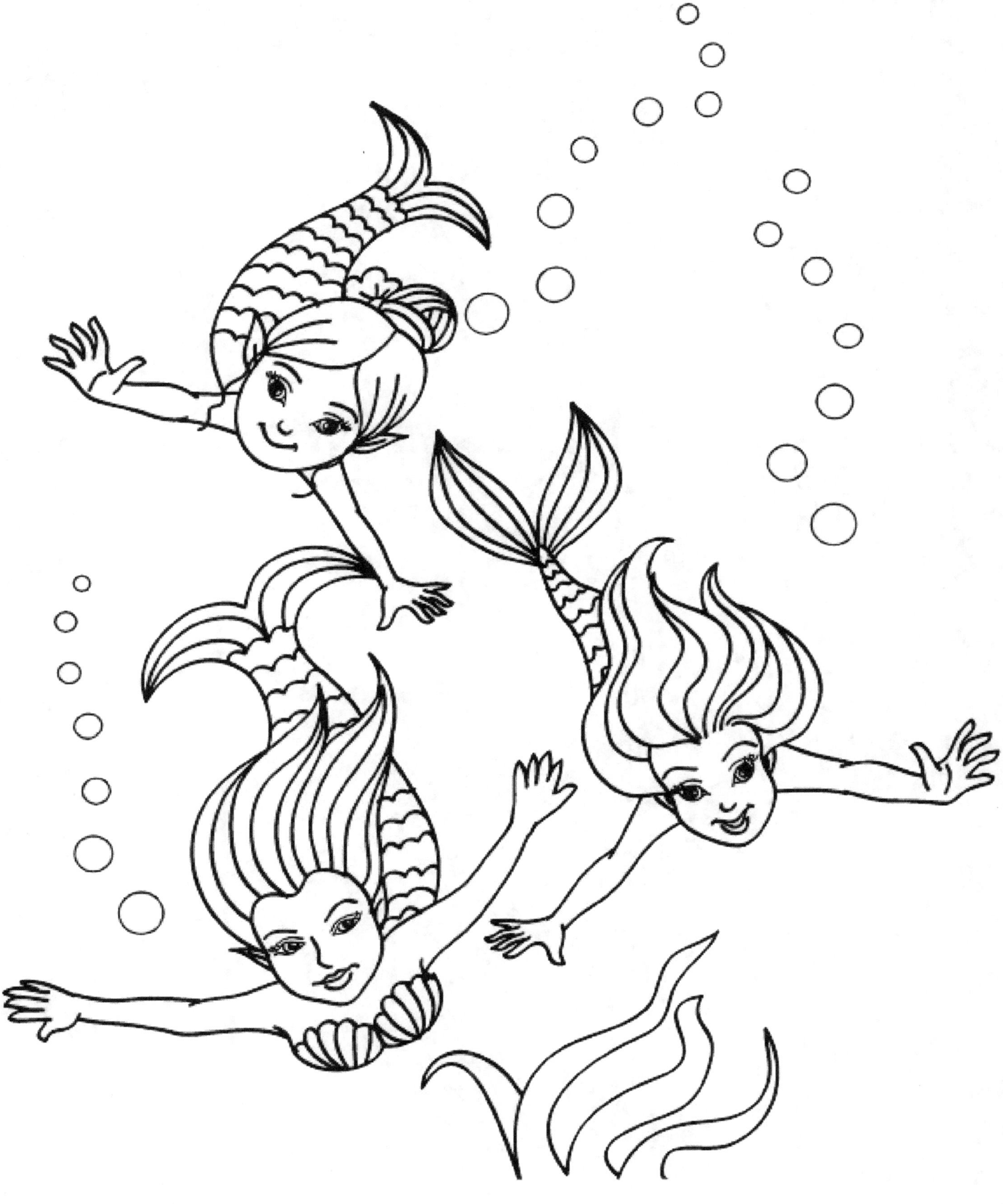

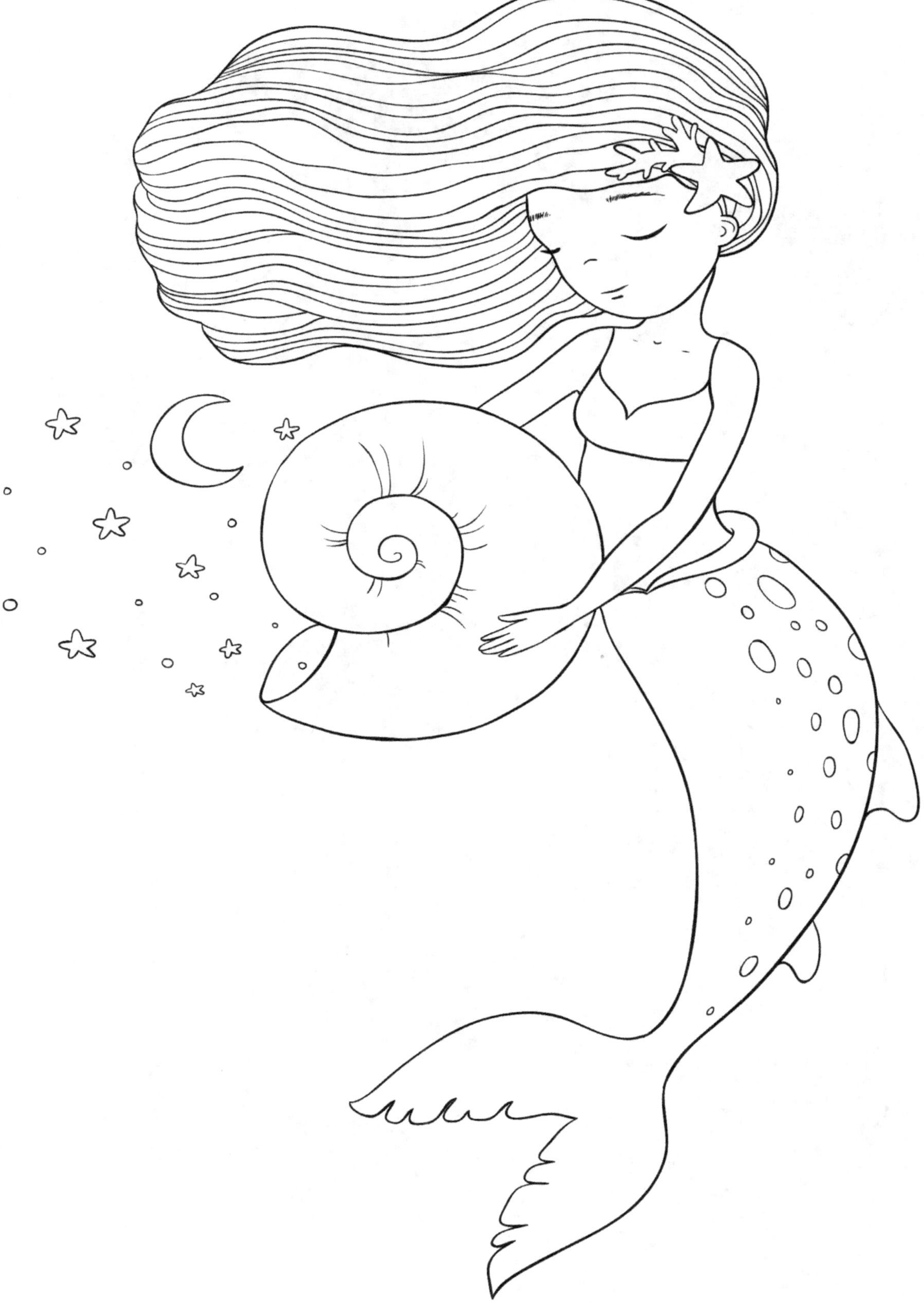

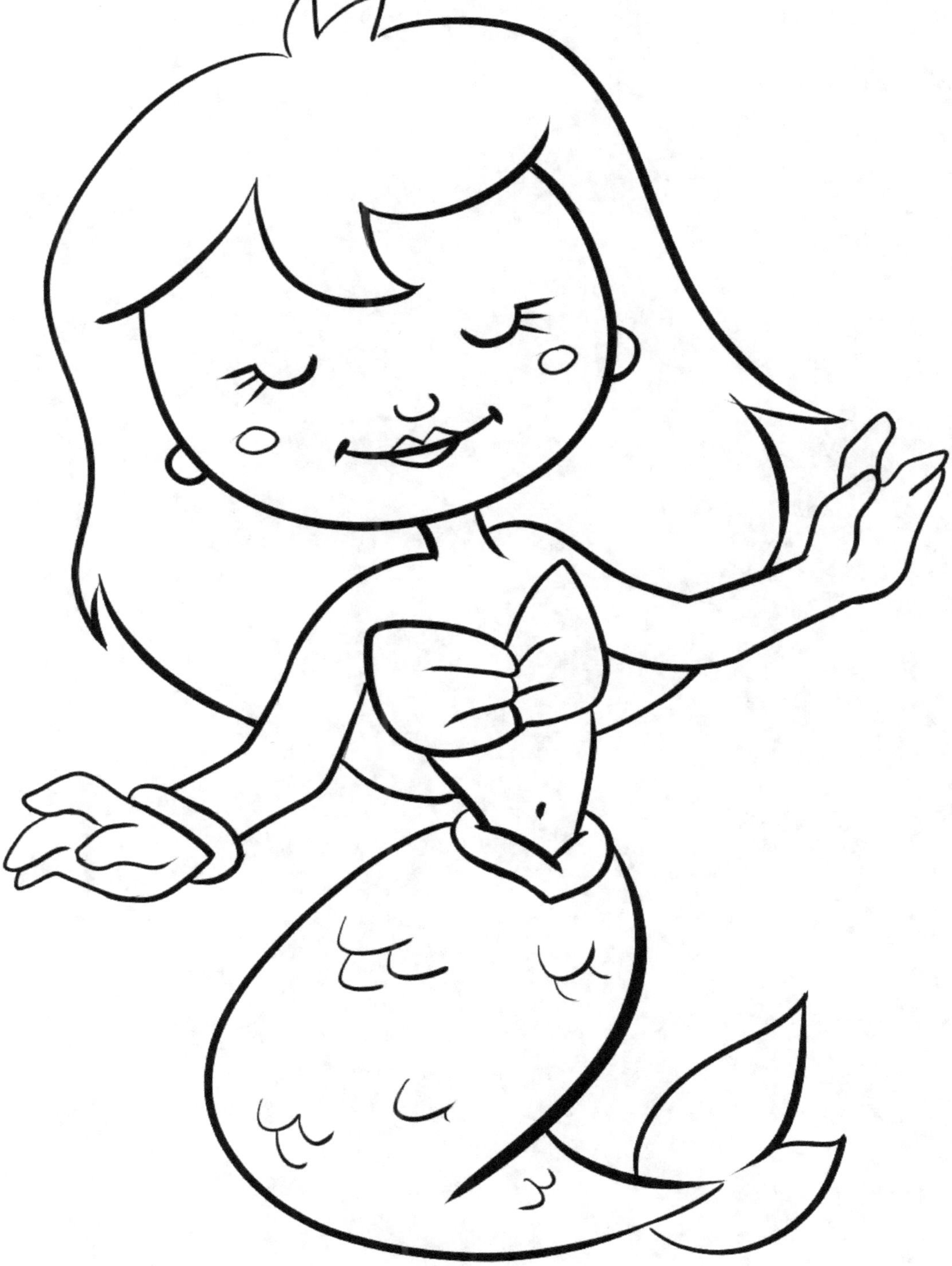

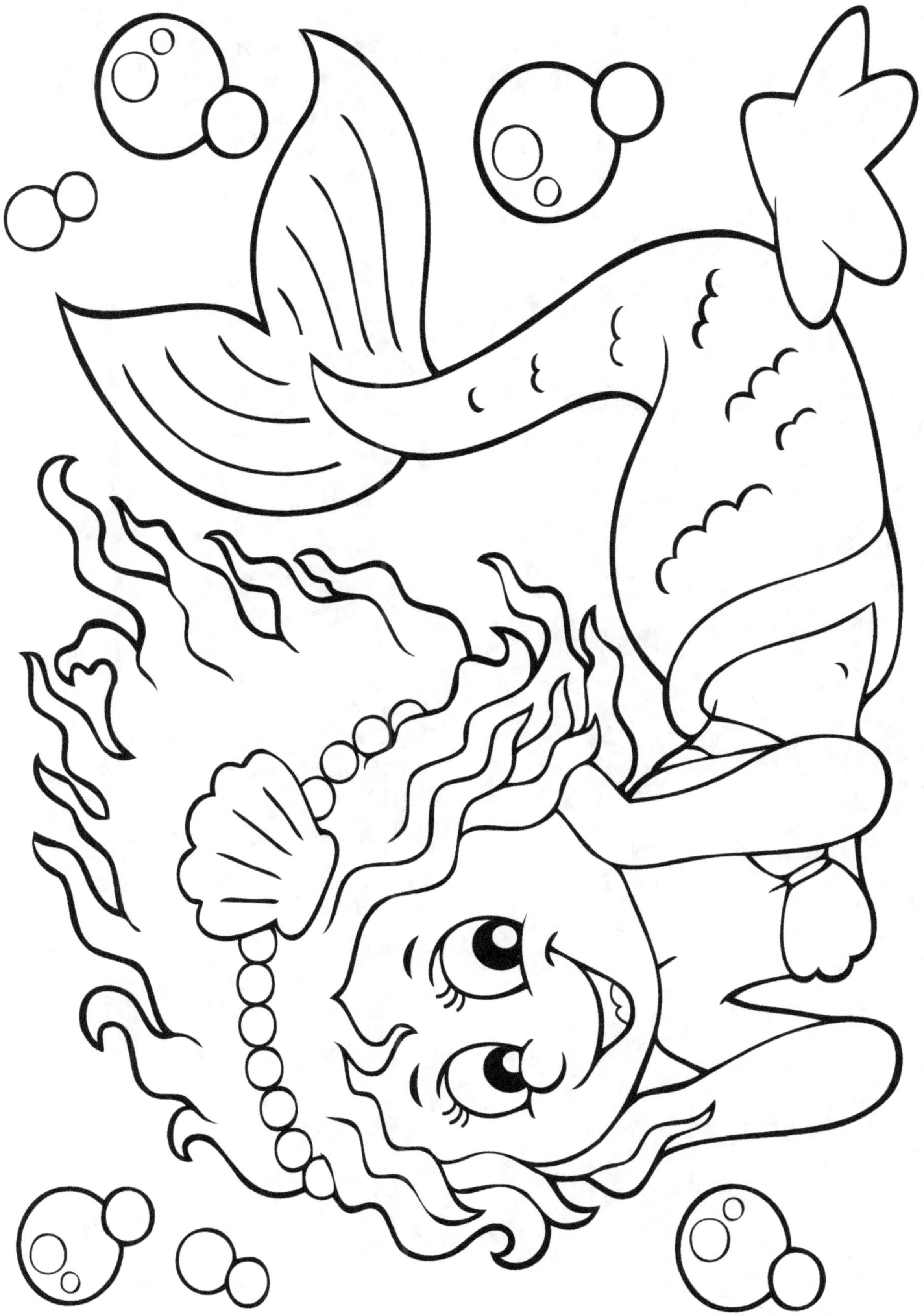

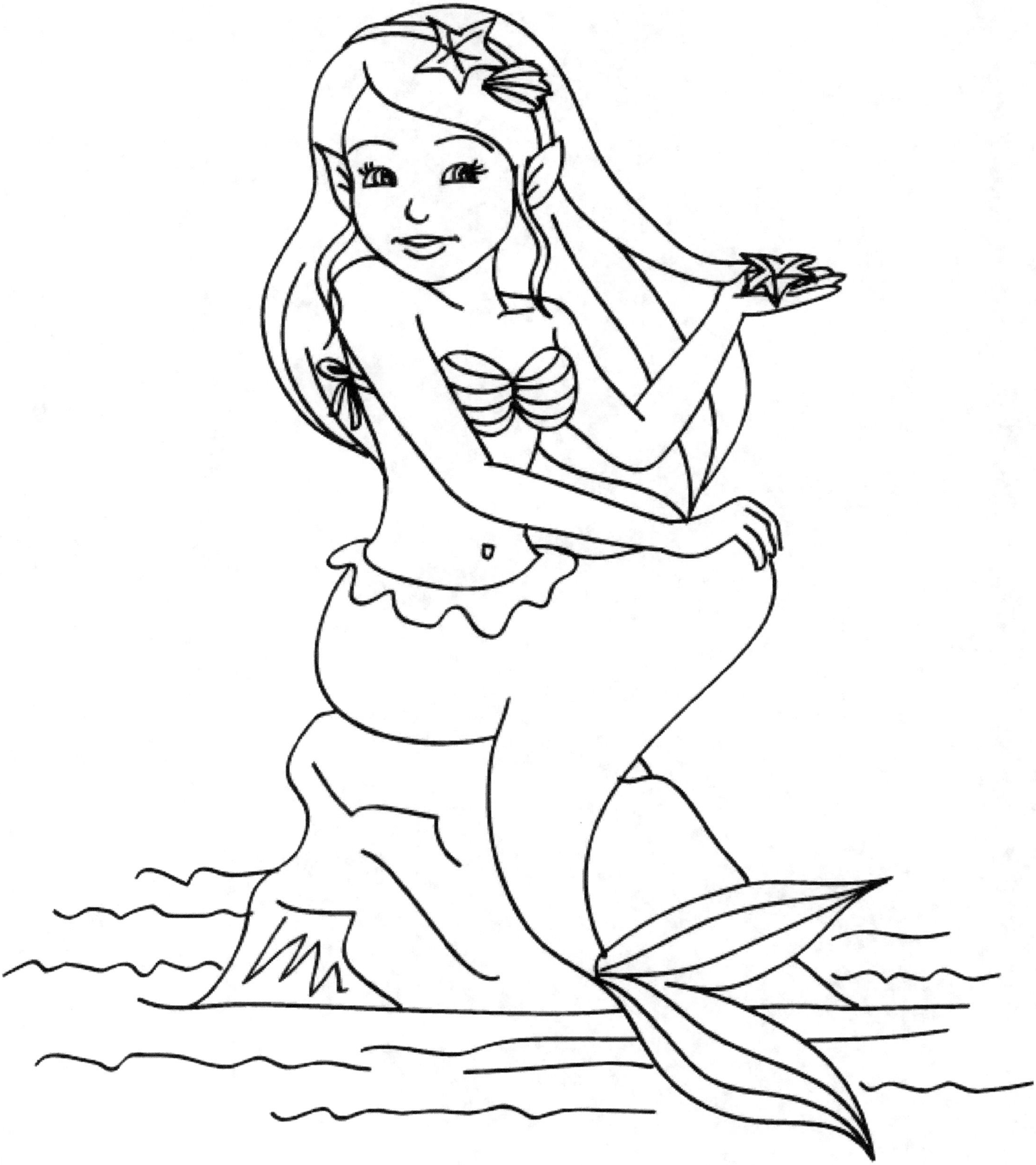

www.ingramcontent.com/pod-product-compliance
Lightning Source LLC
Chambersburg PA
CBHW080620220526
45466CB00010B/3401
* 9 7 9 8 5 3 6 4 2 9 3 7 2 *